# THE HEART OF A CHAMPION

# THE HEART OF A CHAMPION

Inspiring True Stories of Challenge and Triumph

## BOB RICHARDS

Revell

a division of Baker Publishing Group
Grand Rapids, Michigan

Published by Revell
a division of Baker Publishing Group
P.O. Box 6287, Grand Rapids, MI 49516-6287
www.revellbooks.com

Printed in the United States of America

Library of Congress Cataloging-in-Publication Data
Richards, Bob, 1926–
    The heart of a champion : inspiring true stories of challenge and triumph /
Bob Richards. — [Rev. ed.].
        p.   cm.
    ISBN 978-0-8007-3272-1 (pbk.)
    1. Athletes—Biography. 2. Richards, Bob, 1926– I. Title.
GV697.A1R54  2009
796.0922—dc22
    [B]                                                        2009002906

# CONTENTS

# List of Illustrations

# FOREWORD

## DAN GABLE

I first read *The Heart of a Champion* as a high school student-athlete in 1964. What an incredible source of inspiration and motivation! I devoured every page and believed in all it stood for. In addition, anytime I had an issue or problem in my training up to the Olympic Games, I would look to this book for a solution. I always found the answer within the pages of this book. I continued to use it through my collegiate, post-collegiate and coaching years—as a resource for answers and encouragement to stay at the top of my competition. Just like my days as a competitive athlete, I would also turn to this book for answers in helping the individual athletes I coached.

Of course, the years before 1964 were good years for me too, and thankfully strong parenting and support groups led me on my path. Yet, I sure could have used this book during those times to help build an even stronger base of knowledge and certainty. This book has still not left my side and carries me forward in my life. I continue to use it as a tool for motivational speeches and to answer and strengthen my current affairs.

*The Heart of a Champion* and the stories of Bob Richards will never be outdated, for its philosophies and principles hold up eternally. Now more than ever, we need people like Bob who can point us to the ideals and attitudes that lead to success. I'm confident that this fiftieth anniversary edition will inspire a new generation of readers.

Dan Gable,
Olympic champion
and legendary coach

# A Philosophy for Winning

We all want to win. We want to go to the top. We've all got great aspirations, great goals. I'd like to think with you about what I believe to be the ingredients of a winning philosophy, about some great champions I've known in the world of sports who have personified what I think it takes to win. There are certain basic qualities and characteristics you've got to have. Number one: you've got to have a will to win.

I suppose you have all heard this cliché over and over again. It's a phrase used more in sports than elsewhere, and probably used more there than any other statement. The will to win. *The will to win!* As I've analyzed great champions I'm convinced that this is the something that makes the difference between mediocre athletes and great performers in the world of sports. It depends upon whether or not you've got this something deep down inside—this will to win.

It's a will to win, and not just a *wish* to win. I know a lot of people who have what I would call a wish to win. They'd like to go to the top. They daydream about the position they'd like to hold in life. I've seen it in sports. I've seen fellows in locker rooms sitting around dreaming on the benches; you talk to them about their performances, and they've got great dreams about what they'd *like* to be. They tell you their potential, about the heights they could soar to, or the distances they could run, the times they could perform if they would only get out and train and work and do the thing necessary to bring it to pass.

And you find them three or four years later still talking about what they could do if they would only pay the price. Well, it isn't that kind of thinking that takes you to the top. Wishful thinking, or daydreaming, is the kind of escapism that will destroy many a man's greatest aspiration.

Now, I don't mean you dare not dream at all. I think the greatest thing in life is to be able to dream, to have great aspirations, but I think it equally important that you have a will that can turn that dream into reality. You've got to have something within you that is able to translate into concrete practice the idea in the back of your mind.

You've got to dream, yes, but more importantly you've got to have a will that makes that thing come to pass. Let me illustrate by referring to one of my great friends, Dr. Roger Bannister. I don't know how many of you have heard of him. He was the man who astounded the track-and-field world by running the mile in less than four minutes—the first miler in history to do it. If you know anything about running, you know it was a fantastic accomplishment. When I picked up the newspaper and read the headline, "Bannister runs mile in under four minutes," I was flabbergasted. Oh, I'd seen Bannister run, many times. I've seen a lot of great stars run, but I didn't believe anyone would be able to run a four-minute mile for the next twenty years. When I went to Asia recently, I stopped off in London, went out to St. Mary's Hospital and had a talk with Roger about this tremendous feat.

I wish you could hear him describe it. He's the most eloquent describer of what it takes to run that I've ever heard. Having lunch there together, during the week he was finishing his internship at St. Mary's Hospital, we began to talk about how he did it. He told me that in the Olympic Games in 1952, he was terribly disappointed—he was supposed to win, but he wound up in fourth place. He came home more or less chagrined and disillusioned, and he was going to give up running. His medical studies were so demanding that he thought he'd better devote all of his time to preparing for medicine and forget about running.

So he went to his coach and he told him; he said, "Coach, I'm through. I'm going to devote all my time to studying." His coach said, "Roger, I think you are the man who can break four minutes in the mile. I wish you'd give it one last try before you quit."

Roger didn't know what to say, but he went home that night and even as he was studying anatomy, with a pencil in his hand, he began to think about whether or not he might be able to do this thing. Before that night was over, there had crystallized in his mind, in the form of iron will,

11

the determination that before he quit running he was going to try to crack the four-minute mile.

He knew what it meant. He knew he would have to study eight, nine, ten hours a day to get through medical school. He knew he would have to train four hours a day. He would have to run continually to build his body up to the peak of perfection. He knew he would have to eat the best foods. He knew he would have to go to bed early every night and sleep nine or ten hours to let his body recuperate and build up for that great day. Willing to do that, willing to pay the price, for five solid months he went through a routine just like that. And then the day came for him to try for the four-minute mile.

He told me of how he stepped out of the locker room on a cold, blustery day. There was a sharp wind blowing, and as he walked out on the track he could tell that it was going to be slow because five hours of rain in the morning had dampened it. There were very few people in the stands. He talked to his buddies, Chris Brasher and Chris Chataway, after warming up and said, "I'm going to try for the four-minute mile today." They said, "OK, Roger, we'll set the pace for you. We'll do everything we can to bring you in." They shook hands, wished each other luck, and they got down to the mark. The gun went off. Brasher forged out in front, and they started off on the historic race.

Brasher moved out easily and hit the first lap right on pace—57.5 seconds. He had to push hard to maintain the pace because the track was slow, and they hit the second lap in 1:58.2—right on pace. They went into that third lap, the hardest one of all when you're tired and fatigued and when you want to let down. But Chataway now moved into the lead to force the pace, and Roger stayed with him.

They hit the end of the third lap, and of course on that wet track they were both tired. But the time—3:00.5! They were on the way to the four-minute mile for the first time in history.

Roger told me about that moment: "Bob, I don't believe I've ever been so tired. My step began to falter and I felt dead and all of a sudden my head was throbbing and my lungs were bursting and I thought to myself, 'Well, maybe what I'd better do is slacken the pace and just come in to win.'" He started to slow down for a moment as Chataway began to slow; and he described it: "I can't understand it, and I can't communicate it to you, but all of a sudden something welled up within me and it said, 'Roger, if you run until you collapse on that track you're going to make this four-minute mile. If your knees hit the track, you're going to give everything you've got, you're going to do it; you know you can. For five months you've trained. *You can do it.*'"

And so instead of slackening the pace, and with that will crystallizing itself, fighting off the pain, he picked up those knees and began to sprint. He went by Chataway, tore around the curve, and possessed with the madness that only the great ones have, he began to drive with all he had down the backstretch. He let those legs go out, numb and tired, but he let them go. As he hit the last curve his stride began to break again. Describing the feeling he had as he came off the curve, he said, "Bob, I just felt like there was an eternity between the end of that curve and that tape, fifty yards away. But I just closed my eyes and gritted my teeth and forced myself to hold stride, and I went pounding on down that stretch."

He opened his eyes periodically and just before he went into the tape he opened them wide, took that one last step and collapsed in the arms of his manager-coach. The time: 3:59.4! He had done it.

Oh, you can talk about a lot of things involved here. You can talk about the work, the discipline, you can talk about the determination—but beyond all that, there is something down deep in the human heart that you cannot analyze, that you can't pour into a test tube. You can't look at it through a microscope, but it's there—the will to win, the will to accomplish. It's what drove him through those long, tedious strides to the accomplishment that the world is still talking about.

May I tell you about someone else who to me is the greatest all-around athlete I think the world has ever produced? I know you will be astounded when I tell you that I think the greatest athlete of all time is not a man. It's a woman. Babe Didrikson Zaharias. Before you disagree with me, I wish you'd read her life story as it appeared in the *Saturday Evening Post*. This girl was born in Texas in obscure poverty. She resolved that somehow she was going to be great in sports. From the first time she picked up a bat or shot a basketball, she loved sports, and she gave her whole life to them. She had the kind of will that really makes champions. I'm told by her coach that one day he told her that the javelin record was such-and-such a throw. She had never thrown a javelin before but, typical of the Babe's whole mental attitude and philosophy, she picked up that javelin and she went out there and almost broke her back in the process. But she bettered the American javelin throw record *on her first throw!* Have you read her record? All-American in softball. All-American in basketball. Great in swimming. Great in tennis. Great in horseback riding, in archery. She won the national championship in track and field all by herself, winning five first places. She went to the Olympic Games in 1932, and I want to tell you how she trained. She didn't have any training facilities of her own, so she asked her neighbors if she could run through their backyards. And running through their backyards and jumping over the shrubbery, she trained for the hurdles in the 1932 games—and won the gold medal in Los Angeles.

She went on to win another gold medal in the javelin throw. After becoming a star in track and field she went into golf, and she won the National Open championship again and again, breaking all kinds of records for women in golf.

But at the crowning point of her athletic career, with glory and honor hers and having broken every record that it is possible for a woman to break, she was told by her doctor that she had cancer so badly that she'd probably not live through the operation. Can you imagine what a moment like that would be like, at the height of your career, young, strong, famous, to be told that you had cancer and that you were going to die?

The Babe went into that just as she went into everything else, with the will to win, breathing a prayer in her heart that God would help her. With that courage of soul, that determination, that something that no one can describe, she went into that experience, she emerged, she was alive. She was grateful to God for her life, and a year and a half later, still recuperating, still weak, she came back to win the National Open golf championship once again. Then she went through a second cancer operation. She came back *again* to play great golf. She had the greatest asset of human life, a will to win, a will to conquer, a will to go to the top. It's the most important thing you can have, and it's amazing how it can lead people through the most stringent kinds of difficulty.

Secondly, if you're going to be great in sports you've got to have something else. You've got to have inspiration. You think I'm talking in the abstract? What is inspiration? How I wish I could tell you. How I wish I knew what inspiration is. If I did, I would be the greatest psychologist the world has ever known, because even those people who rely upon inspiration most can't tell you what it is. The poets, the artists, the musicians—they don't know what it is. But we can all see it. I've been amazed to see mediocre athletes, fellows drifting along with great potential but never really realizing their full abilities, suddenly inspired by a great coach, or by some great ideal or a sweetheart—something would lift them up and they would do the impossible. In a matter of a few months they would become sensational, and people would wonder what had happened.

I can't describe it or define it, but I'd like to give you one facet of what I think it means when people are inspired. *It's when they see themselves not as they are but as they can become.* It's when they see themselves, not in terms of their weaknesses and shortcomings, their failures and inadequacies, but in terms of what they can be, when they begin to believe they can be what their vision tells them—that's when they're inspired. When they no longer see their weaknesses, but their greatnesses, by emphasizing their strengths they go on to do things they never dreamed of.

May I tell you the greatest story I know of in sports? It will sound unbelievable to you, and I tremble as I tell it, because I know the thing is true. It is a story that goes all the way back to 1920 and to the personality of a fellow by the name of Charley Paddock. I have read his life story and I know how that as a boy Charley had one great burning ambition—to be an Olympic champion. It was the one thing that dominated his thinking, even as a boy.

He went up to his coach one day and said, "Coach, what can I do to become the world's fastest sprinter? What's the secret of sprinting?" His coach replied, "You've got to get your knees high." The secret of sprinting is to pick those knees up and lean forward and reach out. The runners who really sprint are those who get those knees high and drive them like pistons.

Well, Charley Paddock worked on it. He worked on it until he got his knees coming up so high that his thighs hit his chest. And the sports writers tell me that whenever Charley Paddock would start down the track he was a slow starter, but pretty soon those knees would begin pumping and all you could see was just a blur of knees as he would tear down to that finish line. The last five or six yards he would leap off the track, fly through the air, knees still pumping in midair, to hit the tape. He set or tied world's record upon world's record, holding four world's records at one time. In 1920, flying through the air to hit the tape the winner, he claimed the dream of his lifetime when he won the 100 meters in the Olympic Games at Antwerp,

Belgium. He came back home. His inspiration had led him to the heights.

Charley Paddock was a great speaker. He loved to talk with young people. He had one great theme: "If you think you can, you can. If you believe a thing strongly enough, it can come to pass in your life." He was speaking once at East Tech High School in Cleveland, Ohio; he gave a great talk and afterwards he lifted up his hand and said to a thousand high school students, "Who knows but there's an Olympic champion right here in this auditorium this afternoon?" When he finished his speech, a number of young kids came up to talk with him; there was one little spindly-legged boy so touched by what Charley had said that he could hardly talk. His lips were quivering when he came up to Paddock and said, "Gee, Mr. Paddock, I'd give anything if I could be an Olympic champion just like you." Charley reached out and, putting his hand on his shoulder, said, "Young fellow, that's what I wanted to be when I was a little bit younger than you. If you'll work for it, if you'll train, you can become an Olympic champion."

It was the moment of inspiration. That boy was different. Just last week I gave a speech in a high school where a teacher told me that she watched that boy, night after night as he went out, off season and during season, as he ran and ran and trained and trained. In 1936 that little spindly-legged boy, although no longer spindly-legged, went to Berlin, Germany. He won four gold medals. His name is Jesse Owens. Charley Paddock had inspired him; after setting three world's records one afternoon in 1935, he won the 100 meters, the 200 meters, the broad jump, and led off the 400-meter relay team.

But the story doesn't end there. Jesse Owens came back home to Cleveland, Ohio, and as he drove down the street in a great big convertible, the crowds cheered him wildly. He was at the height of his glory; every now and then the big car would stop and he would sign an autograph for a boy. Believe it or not, there was another skinny-legged boy who came up to the side of the car, and putting his hands on the door, said, "Gee, Mr. Owens, I'd give anything if I could be an Olympic champion just like you."

Jesse told me the story himself. This little boy was so skinny that all his friends called him "Bones." Jesse reached out and put his hand on the boy's hand as he said, "You know, young fellow, that's what I wanted to be when I was a little older than you are. If you'll work and train and believe you can, you can become an Olympic champion." Well, that little boy was so inspired he ran all the way home. He didn't stop. Nine years of age. Little old skinny legs. Maybe with his knees knocking. But he ran all the way home and ran up to his grandmother and said, "Grandma, I'm going to be an Olympic champion."

I was at Wembley Stadium in London, England, for the Olympic games of 1948—with 110,000 other people—as the crowd hushed, and as the boys down there, six of them, got set for the 100-meter finals. The gun went off. The boy in the outside lane burst out, drove down the track and hit the tape, the winner. His name, Harrison "Bones" Dillard; he tied Jesse Owens's Olympic record of 10.3. He later went on to hold the world's record in the hurdles. I saw him skim over the hurdles in 1952 in Helsinki in 13.7, to set a new Olympic record. I saw him better one of Jesse Owens's world's records in Salt Lake City, Utah, in the 220-yard low hurdles.

You say it's fantastic? You're saying that it'll never happen again? And I tell you, you're wrong. It'll happen again and again, in boys and girls who are inspired, in young men and women who will catch a vision of what they can become, who will see not skinny legs or spindly legs, but who will catch a vision of Olympic champions. They will rise through training and perseverance and hard work and they'll become champions—they'll break world's records and they'll shatter the marks.

You show me someone who has no inspiration, and I'll show you someone as good as dead. Show me someone with no challenges, no goals, no great aspirations, and I'll show you someone who won't do anything in life. You've *got* to be inspired. Let some great thing pull you up. In living let some great goal, some great ideal, a great coach, some lovely wife, a husband, some sweetheart or friend, a teacher, a minister, let Almighty God inspire you and lift you up to catch a vision of what you can be.

You know, one reason why I think a great deal of Jesus is because, for one thing, He never pointed out the weaknesses of people, never dwelt on their failures and their shortcomings. He always thought of the dream that God had for their lives. Never emphasizing their failures, He simply said, "Go and sin no more. Be what God intends you to be." Lifting people up to catch a vision of what they could be, He changed human life. That's why I think He's the greatest inspiration that has ever hit the human race. Inspiration is vital to greatness in living.

Another point, and this may sound strange to you—*do your level best no matter what.* This may sound like a contradiction in terms, after what I've just said, but would

I surprise you if I told you that some of the greatest champions I've known are guys and girls who never won a gold medal? They were people who, even though they didn't win in the sense of living up to the highest within them, yet they did their best and overshadowed some of those who won the gold medals.

Would I surprise you if I told you that the greatest runner I've ever known, pound for pound, is a little Irishman from Illinois, 116 pounds of solid heart and muscle, 5 feet 3½ inches tall? His name is Johnny Twomey. They used to call him "The Flying Splinter." I've seen that little guy running in races with taller men whose elbows would hit him in the head as he was going around the track. He was that small. But he never gave quarter, and he never asked for quarter. I've seen him push many to record upon record. I've seen others staggering to beat him, as he went on, head held high no matter what place he took.

I saw him in a *Chicago Daily News* meet a few years ago, in a two-mile race, on a board track, with 22 laps to go. The field started off. At the end of half a lap, his shoe came off. Well, if you know anything about indoor running, on a track that's made mostly of splinters, you know that you just can't go on after that happens!

Everyone thought Johnny was out of the race, and a sigh went over the whole stadium. But do you suppose that little guy would quit? Not on your life. One hundred and sixteen pounds of throbbing heart, he kept right on running; absorbing the splinters, he moved up into the pack. At the end of 20 laps he moved out in front, and at the end of 21 laps it looked like he was a sure winner, when a boy from Oklahoma by the name of Forest Efaw, about 6 feet

2 inches tall, began to move up behind him. Talk about Mutt and Jeff on the track—this was it! Forest was making up the range at about eight feet to Johnny's three or four, and as they went into the last lap, he was catching Johnny. Johnny gave everything he had. Forest barely caught him at the tape and surged out in front to beat him by a foot.

Forest Efaw took home the gold medal, but Johnny Twomey took home a heart that was solid gold. I believe, in terms of my own experience, that that kind of thing is sometimes even greater than winning. I would much rather be known as a person who did his level best no matter what, than to claim all the victories and all the records, never having quite fulfilled the destiny that I knew God had for my life.

May I tell you another story? I made a speech in Toronto, Canada, and after I finished speaking, a young boy came up to me. I'll never forget him. He put his right hand up on my left shoulder and said, "Mr. Richards, I know what you mean when you say you can take defeat and bounce back to victory." I'd been emphasizing that sometimes defeats are the substance out of which great victories are made. You've got to learn to take them and keep on going. Then he said, "I had to take a great defeat in my life, and I know you can bounce back and keep going." Well, I was quite naïve and superficial; I put my hand on his and said, "Well, thanks, young fellow, I'm glad to hear you say that," and I patted his hand and turned away, and he walked away. I don't know what it was—some compulsion within me said, "Bob, you've got to turn and look at that boy," and I turned and looked and then it was I realized what it was he was talking about. The left sleeve of his red jacket was dangling loosely; his arm had been cut off at the shoulder, I learned later, in an automobile wreck. And when I saw that boy walking away, I thought, *That guy knows so much more how to take defeat than you ever will.* I started after him, to tell him that I understood what he meant, when George Duthie, the sports director of Canada, nudged me and said, "Bob, you know that that boy who just spoke to you won second place in the ten-mile swim in the Canadian championships yesterday."

I don't even know his name. I dare say that if you looked in all the record books you'd never find his name there, but he's the greatest swimmer I've ever known. With that one arm, doing his level best, reaching out through a ten-mile swim, barely being nudged out, he took home not only the silver medal, but something infinitely greater: he took home character, he took home courage, he took home a winning personality.

I don't think you really win until you live up to that high thing within you that says, "Do your best, no matter what." Grantland Rice once wrote:

> When the One Great Scorer comes to write
>   against your name—
> He marks—not that you won or lost—but how you
>   played the game.

That's why I think the Olympic slogan is so tremendous. The glory of the Olympic Games is not in the victory but in taking part. The essential thing in life is not conquering, but fighting well. This doesn't mean you won't conquer. It doesn't mean you won't find victory. It means that when you do your best, you find the deepest kind of conquering, the deepest kind of victory. Do your best no matter what, and you've found the real secret of winning.

And lastly, take God with you. It's amazing to me, the number of great champions I know who tell me that they pray. They ask God for strength. I was in the national decathlon championship, and after finishing up the ten events, tired and worn out, all of us were walking off the field and one boy, Joel Shankle, national collegiate broad jump champion from Duke University, came up to me. He put his arm around me. We were all tired. He said, "Bob, I want you to know this. I pray as much as you do. I always call on God for strength and health."

Everywhere you go, in sports, you find men like that. I was in Mexico City for the Pan-American games, and I saw a boy who said to a sports writer just before the games began, "With God's help, I'm going to set a new world's record this year." His name was Lou Jones. Nobody gave him much of a chance. He hadn't run a very fast time. But he believed it—with God's help he was going to break the world's record. He got down to his mark. The gun went off and Lou Jones and Jimmy Lea and J. W. Mashburn tore out of their blocks. I've never seen a race like this in my life. They blistered that track, around the curve, down the backstretch. The altitude there was 7,500 feet. And as they came off the curve you could see the effects of running so fast in such an altitude; the boys began to pale. You could see them gasping for air, but there was not one break in stride. There wasn't half a yard between the three of them.

Lou, sprinting like mad, Jimmy right behind him, and J. W. Mashburn right with Jimmy: they were driving down

the straightaway for the last 20 yards, and you could just
see the oxygen leaving them, but they held the stride and
went into the tape. Lou reached out, hit the tape just in
front of Jimmy Lea and J. W. Mashburn and collapsed unconscious on the track.

For forty-five minutes they gave that boy oxygen as he
struggled back to normal. But his time, 45.4 seconds, was
a new world's record in the 400-meter dash. When he
finally got up they took him across the field, and I went
over and put my arm around him and said, "Lou, it was
splendid. I've never seen anything like it." He put his hand
up on my shoulder and said, "Bob, I want to praise God
for helping me run that race." He'd been praying all the
way around the track.

I could tell you of others. Alvin Dark of the Chicago Cubs
tells me he never goes out on the field without taking God
with him. Doak Walker, Otto Graham, Don Moomaw, great
all-Americans, great professional football players: they
say humbly, "Every time I step on the field I pray that God
will help me to do my best." Carl Erskine, Jackie Robinson,
many great stars—all have found this same thing. I think
that there is a great truth in the biblical statement that says:
"They that wait upon the LORD shall renew their strength;
they shall mount up with wings as eagles; they shall run,
and not be weary; and they shall walk, and not faint" (Isa.
40:31). It's a great thing in life. Those happy people, those
people who accomplish, those people of faith, have a deep
religious philosophy. They believe that their lives are under-
girded with a power greater than their own. They believe
that there is a destiny for their lives. Nothing can thwart
them. With God they do great and tremendous things.

So I'd like to urge you—in your work, in your business, in your home—to take God with you; here is a power that can help you reach the heights. It's the greatest ingredient in what I call a winning philosophy. These are the secrets: First, dream great dreams; have a will that translates those dreams into reality, have a will to win. Secondly, let something inspire you, some great goal, some cause, some great challenge; let something or someone inspire you to see yourself, not for what you are, but for what you can become. Do your level best, no matter what. Run the race with the greatest that is within you. Live up to the highest that you have. Do what God has set you to do. And lastly, take God with you. And you know that you'll win and conquer and triumph in life.

Harrison Dillard "turns on the heat" to win in the 100-meter eliminations in the London Olympics, 1948.

The fabulous "Babe" Didrikson displays the perfect form that made her the greatest woman golfer of all time.

Parry O'Brien lets go with the throw that made him shot-put champion—a "heave" of 61 feet, 5¼ inches.

Roger Bannister is near exhaustion—but he has just become the first man to break the four-minute mile. His time: 3:59.4!

Bob Mathias, decathlon champion of 1948, clears the high-jump bar at 6 feet, 1¼ inches (Wembley Stadium, London).

Horace Ashenfelter takes a water jump at the Helsinki Games. He won the final event with a record of 8:45.4.

Ron Delany leads Walter Richtzenhaim (2nd) and John Landy (3rd) to set a new record of 3:41.2 in the 1,500 meters.

The world's finest amateur athletes watch as the historic Olympic flame is borne around the track (Melbourne, 1956).

# The Heart of a Champion

About my only claim to fame is that of being a "pole-vaulting parson." Or, as some others have put it, a "jumping padre." I think the best comment of all is the one made by a sports writer in Cleveland who said that I was the only preacher he knew of who was trying to lift himself into heaven on his own strength.

Be that as it may, I have had a lot of wonderful experiences in this world of athletics. In the past seven or eight years I have had the privilege of traveling throughout Europe and of hobnobbing with a number of great champions. I've had the privilege of rooming with them, of talking with them about their ideas, their drives, what makes them tick. I've had the privilege of watching them as they broke one world's record after another. I've seen more than forty world's records broken in the past few years in athletic competitions. And I've come to believe that what it takes to make a champion in the game of athletics is what it takes to make a champion in the game called life—that life is pretty much made of the same tissue, that one realm is not different from another, that the principles for excellence in one realm are the same as in another, and that what it takes to succeed in the world of athletics is the same sort of heart and soul and quality of personality that it takes to succeed in life.

I'd like to share with you what I've seen in the hearts of a few champions. As I've worked in the world of religion, I know that it applies there. As I've gone on in the field of education, I've found that the same principles apply there.

In other words, what I'm trying to say is that every man and woman needs the heart of a champion. It's a quality of mind, a mental resolve, an attitude that turns a man or woman beyond the normal and the mediocre to accomplishing great things in all walks of life. Perhaps the most important thing that I've seen in the heart of a champion is this mental attitude that refuses to give up, no matter what the circumstances may be.

Now I know people may say that this is rather a trite value, but I have seen it over and over again. I've seen thousands of great potential athletes, fellows with bodies that you would believe would be undoubtedly the greatest coordinated body that a man or woman could possibly want. I've seen fellows with springs in their legs. I've seen fellows with tremendous reaction times and coordination times, but they lacked just a little bit of mental attitude, a philosophy that would help them get over a defeat or a discouraging situation. The difference between a champion and a mediocre athlete is the difference between one who gives up and one who doesn't.

Perhaps the best illustration of this is the story of Bob Mathias. I think Bob Mathias crystallizes in his personality this attitude of mind better than any champion I've ever seen. I saw him in London, England, as a young boy, seventeen years of age. I saw him as a schoolboy achieve probably the greatest honor that any boy could hope to achieve—the Olympic decathlon championship, won under the most adverse circumstances imaginable. I saw that boy go out there and throw the javelin when they had to have a flashlight to show him where the foul marker was. He pole-vaulted under the same conditions; they had to point a flashlight on the crossbar. And I saw that seventeen-year-old boy finish the 1,500 meters in a mud-bespattered condition on a horrible track ruined by the rain; and when he finished as the winner of the Olympic decathlon, probably the most grueling, grinding event of all, I thought, *Could any high school kid hope to achieve more than what this boy has achieved?*

I thought he'd never surpass it, but he did it later in Helsinki, Finland. I saw him go out in the first day of the decathlon; in the broad jump, he pulled a muscle high in his right leg, and if you know anything about pulled muscles in athletics, you know they are tremendous handicaps to overcome. Everyone wondered if Bob would quit, if he would give up. I heard afterwards that when all the trainers and coaches went up to him and put their arms around him and asked, "Bob, what do you think you're going to be able to do? Do you think you'll be able to compete?" Bob reached up, put his hand on his coach's shoulder and said, "Don't worry, coach. Somehow I think I can come through."

Most fellows would have given up; they wouldn't have competed any more. But Bob went out there with that pulled muscle and tried again. He not only came through, but he broke the Olympic record, and broke his own world's record for the greatest single performance of his entire career—all this with a pulled leg muscle.

It's that quality of mind that makes champions. No matter what the situation is, they have the ability to grit their teeth and keep on going. They don't quit. They refuse to give up.

I'll never forget a high-jumper who was 6 feet, 9 inches tall, a fellow by the name of Walt Davis, from Texas. Walt is one of my great buddies, and I had the privilege of getting to know him well. I heard people in the stands make comments such as, "Well, why shouldn't Walt Davis win? He's such a tall boy—who in the world can compete against such a giant?" But what the people who were making those remarks didn't realize was that when Walter Davis, Olympic champion of 1952, was a boy of nine, he had polio so badly that he couldn't move a muscle in his entire body. He went through all the agony of braces, all the struggles to get those muscles to function again. He did practically everything he could to get life back into his legs, and he was successful jumping and training those legs to the point where he has become probably the greatest high-jumper of all time. He jumped over 7 feet recently down in Texas, but a mismeasurement of the ground caused it to be recorded as only 6 feet 10½ inches. But that boy has learned a basic principle of athletic success: *not to give up*. No matter what the circumstances, the champion has a heart that refuses to go down. He somehow comes back and wins the victory when most fellows would throw in the towel.

One of the greatest stories I have read is the story of Johnny Fulton. He's a Los Angeles product and probably one of the finest milers and half-milers that California has ever produced. Many people don't realize that Johnny Fulton, at the age of three, ran across the street one day and an automobile, going sixty miles an hour, hit him and crushed his whole body. His hips were crushed, his ribs were crushed, his skull was fractured, his leg was compound fractured. No one thought he could ever live. His flesh was literally hanging from his bones. No one gave him the chance of ever doing anything in life if he *did* live. One of the greatest stories of all time is the story of how this boy became a champion, how he began to walk, how they massaged his arms and legs with oil every day to get some sort of feeling back into them. Johnny Fulton became a 1:50 half-miler. He became an excellent miler and quarter-miler. He ran the 100 yards in 10 flat, the half mile in 1:49.5, and up to about the three mile with tremendous times.

What was it that Johnny Fulton had? I say he had the heart of a champion. He became one of the world's greatest runners because he had a quality of spirit that couldn't be beaten; no matter what happened, he had a soul that could carry him through. It's that sort of a thing that makes a champion in athletics. It's that refusal to give up. It's that resolve in the mind to go on, no matter what may happen. I've come to believe that it's necessary in life. I don't care what avenue of life you're in, whether it's in selling, whether it's in business or religion or education—whatever it may be—you've *got* to have this mental attitude. How many men and women with enormous abilities and potentialities have never realized the fullness of their nature because they've let something discourage them? They've given up. Right when they were on the threshold of perhaps the greatest accomplishment of their lives, they allowed something to discourage them and consequently didn't go on to break the record.

I read again the story of Abraham Lincoln just about a month ago. Have you read it? Well, read it again and again, because to me it's a story that ought to thrill every American young man and woman—the story of Old Abe, born in obscure poverty, beaten with practically all of the vicissitudes of life. He tried for the Senate five or six times before he ever made it. In business he failed three times, and he was $1,800 in debt when he went to Springfield. That money, then, was "a lot of dough." But Abe Lincoln had the quality of a champion. He didn't give up. Is it any wonder that he became the greatest president that America has ever produced? He had the quality of refusing to give up in any situation.

This is what has made America great. What is the basic philosophy of this nation? I know it's a philosophy of freedom, of liberty, of the great ideals we cherish—but isn't it also in a mental attitude of refusing to give up? Isn't this the story of Bunker Hill, of Valley Forge, of World War I, of World War II? Isn't it the story of the pioneers who went into the wilderness, who laid loved ones to rest in a strange land, who seemed at times unable to go on? They had the quality of heart and soul that made them keep on going. And I believe that is the spirit of America. It's the spirit of greatness; it's the heart of a champion.

The champions I've seen have had another great quality. They dared to believe the impossible. A few decades back they said that a 14-foot pole vault was impossible. They said, "It can't be done; it's physiologically impossible." They maintained that a 50-foot shot was simply beyond the limitations of human strength. They claimed that for anyone to run less than a 4:10 mile or a 10-flat hundred—well, it just couldn't be done.

What is the story behind athletics? It's the story of young men and women who come along and say, "No matter what *others* say, I believe the record *can* be broken." These young men and women, with faith and courage and vision in their hearts, daring to believe the impossible and training themselves to a peak of perfection, have broken every record in the books, and they will continue to break them. Why? It is a mental horizon, a mental vision, a mental attitude of faith that dares to go beyond what has already been accomplished.

I'll never forget seeing a boy in Helsinki, Finland, who I think expresses this beautifully, perhaps better than anyone else I have ever seen. He was Horace Ashenfelter, an FBI man from Pennsylvania. A year before the Olympic Games, a fellow from Russia by the name of Kazantsev had astounded the world by breaking the world's record in the 3,000-meter steeplechase by something like 10 seconds. When Kazantsev broke this record, at first nobody believed it. "Why," they said, "this is Iron Curtain propaganda. No one can possibly run *that* fast. There's a mistiming somewhere, or someone is just trying to propagandize." But Kazantsev did it again. Of course, everyone was flabbergasted and the experts began to scratch their heads and raise their eyebrows, thinking perhaps that this fellow was as great as it was claimed he was.

And so all of them conceded that no one had a chance of beating Kazantsev, that he would win the 3,000-meter steeplechase, hands down. That was the opinion of practically everyone in the world—except a fellow from Pennsylvania by the name of Horace Ashenfelter. The night before the preliminaries of the 3,000-meter steeplechase, a bunch of us were together, and we were really giving Horace a hard time. They call him "The Horrible Horse." He weighs about 150 pounds, and as he runs along he looks just like an old grey mare plodding along. The fellows were ribbing him: "Horace, how is it going to feel to be out there running on the track when Kazantsev is in taking a shower and on his way home?" Someone else said, "Don't be too hard on him. I'll bet Horace will have only three laps to go when Kazantsev is getting his gold medal."

Horace reared up on his elbow as he said, "I don't care what you say. I believe I can go out there and win that race. I know Kazantsev is great; I know he's terrific. But I believe that somehow, if I give everything I've got, I can win that championship." Some of the fellows thought it was really funny, because no one gave him an outside chance. We finally let him go to bed. The next day Horace astounded all of us by running a faster time in his preliminary heat than Kazantsev ran; we began to wonder, and put our tongues in our cheeks. We thought maybe Horace had something that we hadn't figured on. The day of the finals came. You talk about political implications. Here were all the implications anybody could want. East and West, Russia and the United States, and two great athletes, were out there battling for a championship. The gun went off and 70,000 people spontaneously leaped to their feet to watch the greatest race of the Olympic Games. Kazantsev pulled out to an early lead. He was about five yards ahead at the end of the first lap. Horace made up his mind at the end of the first lap that he had to pull up even with that fellow, and that somehow he had to stay with him all the way around the track. He moved up even, hurdle for hurdle, water barrier for water barrier, lap for lap, heart for heart, stride for stride—these two fellows matched all their courage and everything they had. Kazantsev would pull out a little bit ahead, and Horace would grit his teeth and he'd come back and go a little bit ahead, and Kazantsev would come back and *he'd* go a little bit ahead, and Ash would grit his teeth again and he'd come back and *he'd* go ahead!

It was that way all the way around the track for about five laps. At the end of five laps their legs began to wobble, and I thought, as I caught my breath, *Uh-oh, here's where old Ash is going to quit.* I thought surely that this was it, that Kazantsev would beat him. Ash told me afterwards, "Every muscle in my body ached. My feet felt like lead weights, my lungs burned, my mouth was dry. I never felt like quitting so badly in my life, but I just had a faith, a faith down deep in my heart, that if I could somehow keep picking them up and putting them down I could win that race." When all that hurt and pain hit him, he refused to give up; he buried his chin in his chest and he kept on picking those heavy feet up and putting them down. With half a lap to go, Kazantsev began to falter and fall back, and Ash got a renewed determination and began to reach out and dig in even harder. He got over the last water barrier, came to the last hurdle. It looked eight feet high, but he finally got over it and he came sprinting in to win the championship—the greatest upset of the Olympic Games. His time: 8:45.4. He broke the Russian's world's record by over 3 seconds. It was undoubtedly the greatest performance of the Olympic Games. They did not honor him as the outstanding performer of the Olympic Games; that was Zatopek's honor. But to me he was the outstanding American performer at the Games, and that's why they gave him the Sullivan Award for 1952. He dared to believe the impossible.

May I say that I saw America in Ashenfelter, out there plodding along, winning the greatest race of his life? People ask me, "How can you see America in an athlete?" Have you ever stopped to consider the possibility that the American system and way of life is perhaps more beautifully expressed in athletics than in any other field of endeavor? All the competitive element, all the drive, all the pressure, all the fire that makes America great is found in our athletic programs. And when I saw that kid out there fighting off those pressures, when I saw him refusing to give up, when I saw him daring to believe in the impossible, I saw America at its greatest, at its finest.

I believe that the thing that has made America is the dream in the hearts of scientists like Edison and Franklin, the dream in the hearts of politicians who have been statesmen. It's the dream in the heart of practically every person who dares to believe the impossible, who believes that no matter what has been done, men will come along to do yet greater things. Frankly, it's my personal conviction that the greatest things in this world have not yet been done. I don't believe the greatest poetry has been uttered. I don't believe the greatest music has been written. I don't believe the greatest art has been put on canvas. I don't believe the greatest things in industry, in science, in religion, in international relations, in education, have yet been accomplished. I believe that the men and women who will accomplish them are the men and women who dare to believe the impossible. And with this faith and vision in their hearts they will go out to do it. The personal philosophy of life that Jesus gave, which ought to be the philosophy of all of us, is in these words: "All things are possible to him who believes" (Mark 9:23 NKJV).

And then I've seen another great quality. It's the quality that perhaps I've already stressed; it's the ability to be hurt and keep on going. Every champion I've known has had the mental attitude and the physical courage somehow not to quit when he begins to hurt. Probably the outstanding star of the 1952 Olympic Games was a thirty-year-old Czechoslovakian by the name of Emil Zatopek.

Some of you who think you're over the high-water mark at thirty ought to take a good look at this fellow! He won three Olympic championships, setting three Olympic records. He has broken the world's record in practically every event from 5,000 meters up. There is hardly a young fellow who can keep pace with him in the field of distance running. I saw him in Helsinki. I saw him as he went around the track, and as I looked into his face as he came around the curve, I thought, *He can't go two laps.* His face was twisted with pain. He had his right arm doubled up beneath him. He looked as though he'd collapse before the race was over—as though he was going to have an appendectomy right out there on the track.

He went one lap, two laps, three laps, and he began to increase the pace. Everyone began to fall back and they got tired, but Zatopek reached out, running every lap faster than the one before. At the end of about ten laps I thought, *This guy is fantastic. I've never seen anything like him. He comes in from the marathon, a race over 26 miles, still grimacing with pain, with his right arm tucked under his shoulder. And I'm not letting it kid me any more. That guy could run all day long without even batting an eye.*

We talked to Zatopek afterwards. Do you know how long he trains every day? Six and a half hours, every day of the year. Can you imagine it? He works out two hours in the morning, three and a half hours in the afternoon, and in the cool of the evening he goes out and runs for an hour before he goes to bed. Is it any wonder that he has broken every record? He said this to me, and it is one of the most interesting comments I've ever heard: "I run until I hurt; that's when I begin my training program." When most athletes quit and go in and take a shower, that's when he begins to run harder than ever before. He says, "I've learned that if I can just get beyond fatigue, there is a reserve of power that I never dreamed I had, and then I go on to run my best races." It's the ability to hurt and keep on going that has made that fellow the most fantastic runner in all the history of distance running.

I saw it again in one of the American boys, Mal Whitfield. I suppose you've heard of Mal. He was one of the smoothest runners I've ever seen. He was in overdrive when everybody else was shifting from first to second, and he was as smooth as silk. There was only one person in the world who could challenge him, and that was a 6-foot-6-inch boy

from Jamaica by the name of Arthur Wint. You've got to
see Arthur before you'd believe it. He has legs that would
come up to my shoulders—I'm not exaggerating a bit. That
fellow's legs are so long that he looks like a giraffe when
he gets started running. He begins to reach out with those
legs and you think to yourself, "Why, he's completely out
of the race." But at the rate of twelve feet per stride, when
he begins to move, he really eats it up.

I saw Mal win the Olympic 800-meter championship
in '48. I saw Arthur beat him three times straight in 1949,
and I knew this race in Helsinki was going to be one of
those blood-and-guts affairs. Well, Arthur moved out. He
was ahead at the first lap, reaching out with those long
strides. Mal was in about fifth position. Mal moved up on
the outside and took the lead, and Arthur moved right up
on his shoulder. Talk about a race! Mal knew it, Arthur
knew it, and the stands knew it—knew that for 330 yards
and from there on in it was going to take all the heart and
soul that those boys could muster. They dug in. Arthur kept
trying to get beyond him with those big long strides, but
Mal wouldn't let him. He was smooth, but he was beginning to quiver a little because he was tired and worn out.
They came to that last curve. They went around it and
came into the straightaway. Arthur made one last bid. He
was right on Mal's shoulder. He kept trying to get ahead
of old Mal, but Mal just wouldn't let him. I could see Mal
beginning to tie up. I knew that he had run himself out,
that this was the race that was going to depend upon sheer
intestinal fortitude at the end. Mal was tired, but he kept
digging in. The two of them hit the tape just exactly as they
were in the straightaway. Mal won by about a yard, tying

his own Olympic record, 1:49.2. Afterwards I was talking to Arthur and he said to me, "You just can't understand the kind of race it was." And I said, "What do you mean? That's one of the greatest races I've ever seen in my life." He said, "Man, you just don't understand. There was old Mal right in front of me. I knew he was hurting; I could see his muscles tightening up; I could hear him breathing, but I was just so tired myself I couldn't do a thing about it."

It was that kind of spunk that won for Mal Whitfield the Olympic championship. I say it's in the heart of every champ. They can hurt but they don't quit. They keep on going. Life has its hurts, its setbacks, its defeats, its heartaches. No man can meet life in all of its fullness, but he must at one time or another meet hurt and pain and suffering—not only physical but mental pain, spiritual pain, financial pain. In every walk of life there is some sort of suffering and heartache that you've got to face, but the champion is the one who can meet it with a stiff upper lip, with faith in God, and somehow, even with that hurt and pain in his heart, he keeps on going to achieve greatness. I've never read the story of a great man without finding that at one time or another in that man's life he went through days of hurt, and it was the molding influence of the hurt that made the man what he was. It's a great principle for life. It's the heart of a champion.

May I stress one last point? I've seen something else that to me is one of the most beautiful things that athletics can teach a young man. *Champions give everything they've got.* You may not believe this, but I've seen boys go out and run on the track until their knees hit the cinders below their feet. I've seen boys run until they were literally unconscious. Every bit of physical strength and energy they had they poured out in a race or a competition. I've seen boys hit the tape and collapse with their eyes practically in the back of their heads. They give everything they've got, down to the last ounce of physical strength. They also give everything they've got mentally. I've seen fellows with an obsession to succeed, with a goal in mind so strongly, that they could hardly think of anything else. They would concentrate on their form or on a record until they had broken that record, and then and then alone would they do something else they wanted to do. I have watched fellows like Attlesey, Fuchs, Harrison Dillard, Parry O'Brien, and Fortune Gordien as they have concentrated on breaking records for years, and I've seen them pour all their mental will and resolve and determination into accomplishing their goals.

May I also say that I've seen boys, when they've given everything they've got physically and mentally, call on something spiritual that carries them to their greatest performance. I wish I could tell you of all the all-American football players I've talked with, of all-American basketball players, of Olympic champions, of boys in all the realm of athletics who, when they have given all their bodies and all their minds and wills, have yet found something else that enables them to do what they do. Call it God, call it spiritual power, call it something greater than yourself—call it whatever you want—it's there in every personality.

In Fresno, California, I was sitting in the stands with a boy by the name of Parry O'Brien. We were watching some high school boys as they put the shot, as they pole vaulted, as they ran races, and I just casually said to Parry, "What do you do when you put the shot? Do you ever pray and ask God to help you?" Parry looked me right in the eye, 225 pounds of solid man, a brilliant boy, an intelligent fellow; he said, "Bob, a young fellow asked me that the other day, and I told him this, and I'd like to tell you the same thing: 'You can train your body to a peak of physical perfection; you can have it as strong as it is able to be. You can concentrate on shot-putting to the point where you know every minute thing that you're going to do. But when you get into that ring you need something just a little extra, something down deep within you that can give you that extra boost you need for world-record-breaking performances. I always pray to God, because I've found in Him that power that helps me do just that little extra.'"

I watched Parry O'Brien as he went out on the track that night. I saw him get down on his third throw of the evening. He must have prayed, because as the shot left that hand and that grunt left his lips, Parry O'Brien put the shot for a new world's record, 59 feet, ¾ of an inch.

What had he discovered? Not only the lesson of hard work and physical perfection, but also the great lesson that every champion learns: to call on everything he's got, down to the deepest spiritual reserve in his heart and soul. I experienced something like that at Helsinki, Finland. I went to Helsinki with a pulled muscle in my left leg. If you know anything about pole vaulting, as you leave the ground, everything goes out of your left leg. You drive off the ground hard, you bend your hips in and you start pulling up. If your left leg isn't right, you just can't leave the ground properly. I kept waiting for my leg to heal, but it just wouldn't, and four days before the games I had to go out and get in at least a workout. I tried to get off the ground, and it was just like a knife sticking me in the back of my leg. I couldn't even leave the ground.

I'll never forget the psychological reaction that hit me in that moment. I began to think that I was out of the Olympic Games. You can't realize what that is until you train four years for something. In four years I hadn't been out of shape for more than a month, training for the Olympics with all my heart and soul. And then to realize that—well, you were finished. I'll never forget; I walked off that field that day, my pole in my hand, and I never felt so blue and despondent in all of my athletic career. Brutus Hamilton, the coach, came up to me and gave me a wonderful inspirational word when he said this: "Bob, I want to quote a Scripture passage to you. '*All* things work together for good to them that love God, to them who are called according to his purpose'" (Rom. 8:28).

I said, "Thanks a lot. That helps me a great deal." I made my way up the pathway to our living quarters and walked into my room. The other boys were working out, and as I entered the room I happened to see Bud Held's open Bible on the desk beside his bed. You know, Bud happens to be one of the greatest javelin throwers America has ever produced. He's thrown it 270 feet, the greatest performance that any American has ever been able to accomplish. He's studying to be a Presbyterian preacher. When I looked down and saw that Bible, it made me mindful of a resource that I could yet use in the situation. I'm not ashamed to say it. I'd like to recommend it to all of you. In the quiet of the afternoon, in the silence of that room, I got down by my bed on my knees, and I just prayed that God would help me. I've never prayed to win in my life. I never will, because praying to win seems so selfish and so silly, to me. But I've always, in my big competitions, asked God to help me. And that spiritual power has never let me down.

We went out to jump. The crossbar went up to 14 feet, 1¼ inches. Five fellows went over it. It went up to 14 feet, 5¼ inches. A new Olympic record! Four fellows made it. It went up to 14 feet, 9⅛ inches, and Denisenko of Russia couldn't get over it, and Lundberg of Sweden couldn't quite get over it; Don Laz and I were barely able to make it. They moved it up to 14 feet, 11⅛ inches. The wind was blowing. We were getting tired. We had been jumping six hours, and I knew that this was about the end of the competition.

Well, Don missed his first one. I missed mine by a hair's breadth. Don didn't come too close on his second one, and I missed mine again, just by a trickle. Don went up and over his last one and hit it coming down, and I had one last jump. I don't know whether you've experienced this in athletics, but no doubt you've experienced it in business, or had a similar psychological feeling in other situations. You go back there to the end of the runway and look down at the pole vault crossbar and it looks to be about 25 feet high. You begin to get tight, and tense, and this old emotional excitement begins to well up inside of you. Your mouth turns dry and that feeling of weakness hits you all over. You just feel like—well, "I can't do anything."

To make matters worse, 70,000 people in that stadium simultaneously went: "Sssssshhhhhhh." They might just as well have dropped the stadium on me. I started to go, and then I just caught myself and said, "Bob, you won't jump

12 feet feeling like this." And once again in that quietness—it was so quiet I could hear my spikes scratching in the cinders beneath my feet—I just bowed my head, and with my pole in my hand I asked God somehow to help me do my best.

I can't explain it psychologically, but the emotional excitement died down. The tightness and the tension left me, and I began to feel relaxed. That crossbar began to come down to about 15 feet, where it belonged. And instead of feeling weak, I began to feel strong, and my faith began to well up. I began to have the confidence that I could do it. I started to take off—and the wind hit me and I had to stop. I started again and it hit me again. I began to feel a little tight. Once again I just bowed my head and prayed, looked up, saw that Olympic flag and I knew it was blowing in my direction. I knew the wind was with me and I took off, got a perfect take-off and started upward. And here's the unusual thing about the experience. In a split second it dawned on my consciousness what I was doing wrong—I wasn't pushing.

There's the value of prayer for me. *It enlightens you as to what you are doing wrong.* I started up and turned over and it seemed like everything within me said "Push!" I came up off that pole as I had never pushed before. And I cleared the crossbar by about 5 inches. Can you imagine the feeling? Four days before I was about to quit, to give up—and then to look up and see that crossbar on its pegs, to hear the roar of the crowd in your ears! It's an experience I'll never forget. When I hit the sawdust I practically went back up over the crossbar again, and in the next breath I thanked God for helping me. What I found was what a lot of champions have found—that when you've given everything, there's something else you can call on. I don't know what you call it. For me, it's God.

It's there, and it's what makes a champion. I've come to believe that no man will really find the greatest joys in life until he is willing to give everything he's got. There is a strange saying about life that goes like this: "If you don't give, you don't receive." It's only the man who puts himself into something—who pours out all his energy, his mind, his spirit—who reaps greatness and success in life.

Jesus put it beautifully when He said, "Whosoever will save his life shall lose it: and whosoever will lose his life for my sake shall find it" (Matt. 16:25). Whoever tries to hold back shall lose life.

Here's where Jesus is, for me, the Champion of champions in the game called life. Here was One who, no matter what the circumstances, did not give up. When the world collapsed around Him, He maintained His spirit, His ideals, to the very end. Here was One who dared to believe that the impossible could be done, that men could be free from sin, that men could live new lives, that men could reflect the image of God in their personalities. Here was One who didn't quit when He hurt. He went to the cross to live forever, in the hearts of men and in the heart of the universe. Here was One who gave everything He had, physically, mentally and spiritually. He's the greatest inspiration of human life.

# The Melbourne Story

Sports test everything that a person is. Everything that you are comes out when you play the game. Let me illustrate by telling you of one of the greatest experiences of my life. I take you to Melbourne, Australia. I take you to the place where the Olympic Games are being held. I want you to see 102,000 people jammed into a great stadium as 67 flags, representing 67 nations, fly overhead. I want you to feel yourselves one of the 4,000 athletes as they come marching into the stadium—the straight, the strong, the stalwart, representing the finest young people in the world. Be one of them as they line up on the field and then as they take the Olympic oath, one of the greatest oaths of history: "I do solemnly swear that I will take part in the Olympic Games according to the true spirit of sportsmanship for the honor of my country, for the glory of sport."

Be there as they release thousands of pigeons that swirl out in front of a gigantic scoreboard with these words written across it:

## THE OLYMPIC GAMES
## TEND TO BRING MANKIND TOGETHER
## IN UNION AND HARMONY
## WITH THE QUALITIES THAT GUIDE MANKIND
## TO PERFECTION

The pigeons are soaring overhead, symbolizing the aspiration of the world for peace. Then the flags of the world are lowered to half-mast, and the Olympic flag is raised high, with its five interlocking circles symbolizing the five continents of the world merged together into one. Be there as the Olympic band begins to play the Olympic Hymn. They sound it out and you feel a tingle go through the crowd—and then a runner brings in the torch, and a contagion sweeps through a hundred thousand people when they cheer as the Olympic flame is lit. Then to give it world meaning, to speak of world peace, to symbolize the dream of every human being, a 1500-member choir stands up, robed in white, and sings out in the silence of the beautiful day: "*And He shall reign forever and ever and ever. Hallelujah, Hallelujah, Hallelujah.*" It's the Olympic games.

Every aspiration of the human heart is to be found here at this symbolical representation, but the deepest messages come out of the races, of the contests on the track. I wish you could be with those athletes as they march out of that stadium, and as they come back in on successive days to pit the best they have against one another. I wish you could watch them go through the semi-finals, the qualifications, as they come down to the really dramatic moment—the final of the Olympic Games. I wish you could be there and feel with them what they feel as a voice breaks out over a loudspeaker system, "Get on your marks!" You see eight men or women go up, some of them literally trembling all over, some of them breathing a prayer that God will give them strength to do their best, and then in the quiet, there is that terrific command, "Get set!" You see them as they come up and then "*pow*," that gun goes off and you see them plunge out of their blocks, down the straightaway, around the curve, down the backstretch.

When you see that you are seeing life; all the drama of human existence comes out in these great races. The striving for records, the striving for victory, the hurt, the pain, are all there. The qualities that drive these contestants on to victory are the self-same qualities that men need and women need, in living.

I want to talk about Melbourne—about some of the races, and some of the values there, in the belief that what took place there should take place in every human heart. And first of all is this: if there was one thing I saw, it was a burning desire to win. I say this unequivocally: those boys and those girls who won in Melbourne gained their triumph because they had a little bit more of the thing called desire.

I can't pour it into a test tube. I can't define it in words. The best way I can communicate it to you is to give you an illustration of the 800-meter race. I wish you could have seen it: 100,000 people literally tingled with anticipation as eight runners went down to their marks—five of them held or came close to setting world's records at one time or another. How would you like to go down to a mark knowing that the fellow next to you could beat you by six inches? Or that if you beat him, you'd have to run down to the last bit of strength in you? When those fellows went down you could just feel the pressure descend upon them, and the crowd grew quiet, the gun went off, and you could see them lunge out of their blocks, wide-eyed.

For the first fifty yards they run on emotion, almost on pure adrenaline. They don't even think. And then all of a sudden they begin to think and the strategy comes out. Arnie Sowell took the lead. The flawless runner from Pittsburgh began to move out in front. He had a strategy to set a pace so fast that he would kill everybody else off in the race. When he came around the curve, up the straightaway, a stiff wind was blowing against him, but he didn't let it slow him down one iota. He just picked those knees up and ran with everything he had. They sounded the bell at the end of the first lap. Around the curve, and the crowd roared even louder; down the backstretch he broke into a sprint, running with everything he had. That was his mistake. And you only make one mistake in Olympic competition. You only make one.

Right behind him was Tom Courtney, of Fordham University. Behind Courtney was Boysen, the world 1,000-meter record-holder from Norway, and right behind him was Johnson, the dark horse from Great Britain. Behind Johnson was Lonny Spurrier of California. These five world-rated runners came into the curve, 200 yards left in the race, every boy tired but every boy giving everything he had.

At the curve, Sowell began to wobble. The pace was too fast, his legs just wouldn't take it. Courtney passed him right in the middle of the curve, went around him, and as Courtney came off the curve, three boys went around Sowell at the same time. They were right on his shoulder, and just as they hit the straightaway a terrific gust of wind moved down and hit them, and Tom ran completely out of gas.

Some of you old-time athletes know what that feeling is—that sickening fatigue when your head is throbbing, and you feel faint and your legs are numb and your lungs are burning, and your mouth is dry. Everything within you wants to go on. You hear the roar of the crowd. You see the judges. But the body just wants to cave in. As the Bible puts it, "The spirit indeed is willing, but the flesh is weak" (Matt. 26:41).

Tom hoped everyone was as tired as he was. He tried to hold on, when all of a sudden Johnson of Great Britain forged around on the right, went out in front by about two yards and began to sprint as the crowd went even wilder. They were on their feet stomping, yelling. Tom told me later that seeing that fellow out in front of him, all he could think was, "I have to win this race." He *had* to. And with the desire that makes one great, he picked those tired knees up and began to find his way back at the rate of about an inch per yard. He began to close the gap on Johnson; with ten yards left he was even with him. You could hardly hear yourself think.

You talk about the personification of human desire! Here was a fellow almost unconscious, his head back, his eyes closed, his teeth set. He would have been a terrific advertisement for Pepsodent, because every tooth in his head was bared and with every muscle rippling he drove toward the tape, lunged out and hit it—and collapsed. He beat Johnson by six inches, to win.

But here's the point: he couldn't even stand up after the race was over. He was so tired he couldn't go out to receive his gold medal. They postponed the victory ceremony for an hour. Ducky Drake of UCLA told me that they had to revive Tom five times. He almost lapsed into unconsciousness.

Why do I tell a story like this? Because nothing I know of portrays desire better than a race like that. It is the kind of desire that takes a person to triumph in life. It's a far cry from the flippant remark, "I think I'll go out and win a gold medal," or "I think I'll enter the Olympic Games." It isn't that easy. To win the great ones, you've got to train thousands of hours. There is only one coin that will pay the price of training—desire. To win the great ones, you've got to put out all the way down to your toenails. There is only one thing that will do it: a burning desire to win. You've got to have enough desire to pour on the extra bit of effort: *that* is the thin margin between victory and defeat. Only one thing will do it: a burning ambition, a compulsive desire.

I have talked to people all over the world about what makes a champion, and I've heard some of them say, "It's just sheer hard work. If a person's willing to work hard, that's all it takes." Others say, "No, it's great coaching. If you've got a good coach, a coach will pull you out, and you are bound to be good." Others say, "No, it's the opportunity. Give a man an opportunity and it will make him great. It's the circumstances that make men."

Others say, "No, it's sheer God-given, naked, raw potential. If you've got the ability, that's all you need." Others say, "No, it's inspiration, it's encouragement, it's the pat on the back." I don't minimize any one of these things. You've got to have all of that. They are all important, but there's something far more fundamental. You show me a boy or a girl with a desire to win, and I'll show you a person who will work hard the thousands of hours it takes to win. Show me those who want to go to the top, and I'll show you people who will take coaching. They will welcome it. They will beg for it. They will use every God-given talent they have to its utmost. They will drink in inspiration, but if they lack desire they won't work. They won't take coaching. Opportunities? They'll never see them. Talent will lie dormant within their breasts. Inspiration will fall upon them like water on a duck's back. Life requires an inner response. The Bible claims that the issues of life come out of the *heart*. You've got to have a burning desire in your heart. It just doesn't come out of the blue. It emerges when a fellow begins to think about a world's record, when he begins to entertain great ideas, great concepts, great goals. And it's when those concepts and goals become an obsession in his mind that they crystallize into a burning ambition to accomplish them. That's where desire originates.

And that's when a fellow pays the price. I have come to agree with the hymn that says:

> Prayer is the soul's sincere desire,
> Uttered or unexpressed;
> The motion of a hidden fire
> That trembles in the breast.

If you want to be great in sports, or in life, you've got to have an inner motivation. Something to drive you. I call it desire. You call it whatever you want, but I've never seen a race won without it.

Secondly, you've got to have a fighting heart. I don't mean fighting heart just in the mere athletic sense, as it pertains to sports. I mean it as it touches all of life, as it goes down into the deepest aspects of living. I don't believe there's a greater thing in the world to have than a fighting spirit, the kind of an attitude or set of the mind or will that can meet obstacles and difficulties, and rise above them—the kind of an outlook on life that says no matter what happens, I am going to try to transform it into good.

In the realm of sports, some of the greatest stories have come out. I wish you could have been in Melbourne and seen Harold Connolly throw that hammer. Perhaps you read about this boy who fell in love with a Czechoslovakian girl and who married her; the international romance is a wonderful story. But greater than that story is the story of a boy who struggled, and who reached the top. In Melbourne his story had its culmination. If you had been there and seen this boy waving at 100,000 people in triumph, you would have thought it was the most glorious day of his life. There was a Russian on his right, a Russian on his left. He held a gold medal in his right hand. He was the champion of the world, and he was waving as he received the ovation of the crowd. If you had seen his right arm, you'd have thought, *Look at that man! He's got everything.* His bicep was eighteen inches. And talk about a grip! You shake hands with that guy, and all you pull back is broken bone and pulp. I have never felt a grip quite like it. But underneath the blue USA uniform, dangling loosely at his side, was a crippled left arm, two-thirds the size of his right. He broke it thirteen times when he was a child, and it never healed properly. This could have beaten him. It was literally a stump that was crooked, but Harold Connolly had the something I'm trying to describe. He did push-ups with his arm; he lifted weights; he did chin-ups. He did everything in his power trying to build up that arm. I wish you could have seen his fifth throw in Melbourne. As he stepped into the seven-foot circle, 100,000 people waiting, he looked out over his shoulder at the two Russians who had broken the Olympic record. They were way out ahead of everyone else. He had fouled once. Just two more throws was all he had.

He put that crippled left hand on the handle of the hammer, got his right hand on top of it, and just before he threw, he lifted his eyes and prayed that God would help him do his best. And then with that 16-pound ball whirling around his head at a terrific rate of speed, he leaned back at about a 45-degree angle and let it go with a terrific grunt. Have you ever heard 100,000 people suck in air at the same time? I stood there on the field, gleaming white clouds and blue sky in the background, and it seemed like an hour that that hammer hung in the air—and then finally came down *kerplunk!* An instantaneous roar arose from that vast stadium, and I watched him. In unbelief at first, a smile went across his face, and he lifted his hand in triumph.

When you see something like that, you see more than just a hammer-thrower. You see life. What that boy did in sports with a handicap is what people can do in living—in every difficult circumstance—if they can respond the way this boy responded.

I wish you could have been in the swimming stadium and watched Shelley Mann receive her gold medal. The American girl stood there, tall, straight, beautiful. An American girl was on her right, an American girl on her left. Tears were running down her cheeks. You'd probably have said, "Just another victory ceremony." Some of the fellows would probably have been saying, "Boy, look at that gal! She's got everything." And she did. She had everything.

But a week before that time, a bunch of us were at dinner in the Olympic dining hall. Conversation was running fast, back and forth across the table. Shelley Mann sat opposite me. The conversation finally turned to Shelley as she told her life's story. She told how, when she was five, she had polio so badly that she could hardly move a muscle in her body. She went into a swimming pool, not to become the champion of the world, but just to get a little strength back in those feeble arms and legs. At first she was held up by the buoyancy of the water. She told me she cried the day she lifted an arm out of the water. It was a major triumph. Her ambition was to swim thirty feet, the width of the pool, and she worked laboriously through the months, through the numbness and pain to get across that pool. Then she wanted to swim the length of the pool. She swam two lengths, three lengths, four lengths. That girl held eight American records; she became the greatest woman swimmer in America. In Melbourne I saw her in the butterfly stroke, the most difficult stroke of all, as she reached out and pulled her body through that water and hit the end of the pool and triumphed. She beat Nancy Ramsey of Seattle by a foot. If you had seen her standing there, clutching a gold medal—the girl who at one time couldn't even hold her hand up—you would begin to understand what I mean when I talk about a fighting heart. Those with fighting hearts don't let anything beat them. They struggle on. They transform difficulty into greatness.

It's the kind of a thing the Hungarian boy had when, in 1952, he looked down his pistol barrel and split the bull's-eye again and again and again. He just couldn't miss. He too won a gold medal with that perfect right hand and eye, and coordination. Six months later, he lost his right arm. And in Melbourne he came back with his *left* hand, and split the bull's-eye again and again and again, three and a half years later, to win his second gold medal with his left hand.

You can't beat them. They've got something within them that, no matter what happens, enables them to rise above it. They have a champion's heart. It's what Glenn Cunningham had when his legs were so terribly burned that the doctors claimed he'd never walk. He became one of the greatest runners of history. It's the kind of thing a little girl had—they were saying of her, in pity, "She will never use her legs again"—when she dazzled the experts with what she did with those legs when she won the world's figure-skating championship. Her name was Tenley Albright.

It's a Buddy Davis, struggling through the braces, when they said, "He'll never be normal." He wasn't. He high-jumped seven feet and became one of our greatest pro basketball players. It's a Ben Hogan, struggling through a horrible automobile accident, and coming back to win the National Open.

It may sound strange, but many champions are made champions by setbacks. They are champions because they've been hurt. Their experience moved them and pulled out this fighting spirit, making them what they are. Sometimes, in life, God gives us a difficulty in order to bring out the fighting spirit. Everything that happens to you can happen for good, if you have this spirit. If you forget everything else I say, I hope you will remember this: *life does not determine a champion; a champion determines life.* The Olympic Creed says, "The glory of the Olympic Games is not in the victory, but in taking part—taking part like a man." The essential thing in life is not in the conquering, but in the fight.

Thirdly, strive for perfection. I can tell you why these men and women break world's records. I can tell you why they bring home gold medals: it is because they are never content with mediocrity. No matter how high they've gone, they want to go higher.

If they have one little flaw, they will work hundreds of hours to eliminate it for they know that a flaw can beat them, and they keep striving to perfect their form. The best illustration I know of this is Bobby Morrow, of Abilene Christian College in Texas. I watched him in Melbourne as he trained. He'd go down to his mark, and it was so odd by contrast to watch him starting with some of the other fellows. The starter would say "Get set," and they would all try to beat the gun. Have you ever watched fellows try to beat the gun? They are jerking, going forward, coming back. Bobby Morrow, by contrast, would just wait there without a tremor. He wasn't trying to beat the gun at all. Just *waiting* for it, every time. Some would be rolling forward, trying to get out just as the gun hit. I met coach Oliver Jackson, and I asked him, "Why is it Bobby doesn't try to beat the gun?" He took me by the arm and said, "Bob, in his whole competitive career, Morrow has never once jumped the gun. He thinks it's unsportsmanlike, un-Christian, to get a jump on a competitor." I'd been in sports for ten years, and I had never thought much about that. Bobby preached to me one of the best sermons I ever heard preached, and he didn't even say a word. The strange thing about it is, he was better off. All these fellows who tried to beat the gun leaned forward until they were off balance so that when the gun went off they couldn't run. Morrow, on the contrary, reacted instantaneously. His knees would come up, those arms would pump and he was running. He told his coach, "Watch me from behind. If there's the slightest tremor, tell me." Every step had to be perfect for Morrow, in perfect balance. His coach would watch him and say, "On your third step there was a little bit of a tremor." He worked until that tremor was gone. He measured his step to the quarter of an inch for 25 yards. Every step had to be perfect.

I watched him exchange the baton in the relays with Thane Baker of Kansas. Thane would come up and give him the baton, and Bobby would take the thing and roar around the curve and up the straightaway. His teammates would yell, "Pretty good, fellows. Wonderful. Forget it. It's good enough." And Bob would come back and put his arm around Thane and say, "Pretty good, but not good enough. We've got to perfect it." They worked by the hour on the baton exchange. I watched him lift that hand when the gun went off and he came up out of his blocks; a couple of them had beat him out of the blocks, but at five yards it was all over. He had the perfect running form. He went by them, went into the tape running easily to win his first gold medal.

I watched him come around the curve and blaze down the straightaway leaving everyone behind him, even with a slightly strained muscle in his leg—into the tape, lower jaw drooping, he was so relaxed. *Two* gold medals. I watched him take the baton from Thane Baker. As Thane gave it to him they didn't lose a split second. It was a perfect exchange. Round the curve, up the straightaway, into the tape again—his *third* gold medal, the last one a world's record for himself and his teammates. If you knew how hard it is to win just one of those gold medals, then you'd appreciate what I'm telling you. *Three gold medals.* And why? *Sports Illustrated* beautifully defined it: "Bobby Morrow is 41 seconds of blazing perfection." Forty-one seconds of perfection. That's what makes them great.

I'll never forget the tower diving events. Have any of you tried to go off a 35-foot tower into the water? Let me tell you something. You haven't lived until you have. You just haven't lived at all. I used to go out with the team. I'd watch these men and women as they went off the high board to do three and a half flips and split the water like an arrow. They are going 35 miles an hour when they hit the water. If they miss, they can black their eyes. They step out into space literally, lean back and tuck, and drop in like a bomb, straight down; they come out of it and somehow always split that water clean. It looks so easy, and I thought, *I ought to be able to do that. That's only twice 15 feet or so.* And so one day I got my suit on and jauntily made my way up the ladder, going through all the kidding from my buddies down below. They were waiting for the kill.

I got up there on top and everything was fine—until I looked down. When you try it, don't look down. It's five times higher, psychologically. I just froze. I couldn't believe it. Finally I got courage enough to look out over the edge and find the pool, and I would have gone right back down that ladder again but for the fact that there were a bunch of girls down there watching me. I *had* to jump. I had to prove my masculinity. I gulped hard and went off.

It wasn't so bad as I thought. The first five feet were wonderful. You'll enjoy it. It's a marvelous view. But I warn, watch out for the last 30 feet. It's hard to put into words but it's something like this—oooooosssssssh! And then all of a sudden, *Boom!* as you hit the water. My arms collapsed, my head almost flew off. When I came up out of the water, I was *so* glad that everything was still there.

My appreciation grew by leaps and bounds for those high divers, especially for a woman named Pat McCormick. She would go off the board, do two and a half flips forward, then a double twist, splitting the water perfectly. Every time she did it, we all roared our approval. We'd say, "Perfect, Pat. Wonderful." She'd come up out of the pool and the coach would put his arm around her—I should tell you that he happens to be her husband—and say, "It was a good dive, but your toe wasn't quite pointed. Your tuck wasn't quite right. You went a little askew; you weren't quite straight." The woman would listen patiently as her husband outlined the errors in the dive. She'd go back up that ladder and—I'm not exaggerating at all—she'd go off that thing twenty-five or thirty times, just working on pointing her toes. Can you imagine it? I was so grateful that I had all ten of mine left, and she was worrying about pointing them. I never went to the pool without seeing Pat training, working for perfection. She won two gold medals at Helsinki. Six months after giving birth to a baby boy, she won those same two gold medals again. It was unprecedented in history. She took the Sullivan award. Her secret comes from her own lips: "With every dive, I strive to be better." Parry O'Brien says, "With every shot put, I strive to throw harder." That's why they go *beyond* the maximum. That's why you can't lick them. They are striving for perfection. You may think it's exaggerated, but in Olympic competition, I've seen boys lose out by a chin in a 100-yard race. I've seen boys in the shot put throw the shot and lose *by a quarter of an inch*. I've watched a man in the broad jump go off a toe-board, hit that toe-board perfectly so he thought, and go a foot and a half out beyond everyone else, land in the pit, thinking he's won—only to turn around, and see a red flag wave. The boy had fouled by an eighth of an inch. That's all. *Just an eighth of an inch*. It cost him the championship of the world. He never placed. Gary Tobian went off the 35-foot tower in ten almost perfect dives. On one dive his feet came apart for a split second; he pulled them back together, went into the water, but he lost to Capilla of Mexico by 1/100 of a point. You lose one like that once, and it will dawn upon you how important little flaws are.

I hope you'll forgive this personal reference but—would you like to know by how much I won two Olympic gold medals? By two inches once, and an inch the next time. Don't tell me those little flaws don't show up, because they do! I have missed the world's record I don't know how many times, because my elbow would come through and knock the crossbar. Once my thumb knocked it off.

You don't win until you conquer the little flaws. You don't beat these great ones until your form is perfect. This is true in all of life. A flaw in a product can ruin a business. A personal failing, a little one, can ruin a person's life. Don't be content with mediocrity—strive to live up to the greatest within you. Live up to the greatest challenge of all time: given two thousand years ago, it's still the greatest challenge of history: "Be ye therefore perfect, even as your Father which is in heaven is perfect" (Matt. 5:48).

And lastly, I saw a spiritual dimension at the Melbourne Olympics. You don't see this in the newspaper write-ups. You don't see it on the gigantic scoreboard listing the victors or the losers, or in the statistics. You don't hear it in the tumult and the roar of the crowd. You don't get it in the unofficial point standings, or in propaganda. You only get it if you know some of these athletes personally. You get it from a Bobby Morrow who says, "I've never run a race in my life without praying that God will help me do my best." You see it in Milt Campbell on his way to a new world's record. He's got seven beautiful scores, and on the eighth event he misses—by two feet. He comes out of a pole-vaulting pit, hitting his hands together and saying, "How could I do this to myself? How could I have done it?" He stands 6 feet 3, weighs 205 pounds. Tears are running down his cheeks. He thinks he's beaten. With his shoulders slouched, he walks up the field, dejected, into the locker room. I went in a few minutes later and I saw Milt there, sitting with his head in his hands, about to give up, when all of a sudden he slipped off the bench, and he prayed, "Oh God, if you will help me come back, I'll give You all the praise and all the glory." His shoulders straightened and he went back out on the field, took the javelin, roared down the javelin runway, planted his feet, bent in and let it go—about 10 feet farther than he had ever thrown it before. He ran his fastest 1500-meter to hit the tape, breaking Bob Mathias's Olympic record.

You get it from a Delany of Ireland. In a 1500-meter race, Brian Hewson comes off the curve, and the boy from Ireland is right behind him. Over 100,000 people are watching it. You couldn't have gotten another person in that stadium. All of them are roaring for John Landy, who is coming up fast. The boy from Ireland is stoical, expressionless; his knees pumping like pistons, he drives down that straightaway into the tape to win the championship of the world. And with 100,000 people roaring, he kneels down in the middle of the track and with his head in his hands, he thanks God for the victory.

A boy skims over the hurdles and beats Jack Davis by four inches, and as you go up to congratulate him he whispers in your ear, "I was praying all the way." It's something you find in a Harold Connolly, in a Pat McCormick, in a Shelley Mann, a Tom Courtney; it's in the great ones, this spiritual dimension.

I have always prayed in competition, not to win, but that God would help me do my best. I have found that when you pray, instead of being all tight and tense, you relax. Instead of thinking negatively, you think positively. Instead of being all dissociated, you are integrated—every muscle and bone is working for you. I don't quite know what it is, but when that divine dimension touches your life, the greatest within you comes out.

What happened at Melbourne should happen to everybody. We should all discover desire, and fighting hearts, and a striving for perfection, and a spiritual reality. Each of us is running a race, before the greatest crowd there is—humanity. We are running it before the greatest judge—God! My hope and my prayer for you in your life, in your community is that you will so run your race that you can say, with the great athletes of the spirit, "I have fought a good fight, I have finished my course. . . . Henceforth there is laid up for me a crown of righteousness" (2 Tim. 4:7–8).

# ATHLETICS AND LIFE

There is a definite relationship between what a man or a woman believes in his or her heart and what that man or woman is able to do with his or her life. Particularly is this true in the world of athletics. Some of you may be thinking, "Oh, athletics is a physical world, a world of grime and bone and pounding lungs and aching muscles." That's all a lot of people think it is—just a world of physicality.

I've come to see a lot more than just flesh and blood in athletics. I've come to see heart and soul and mind and character. I've seen some of the greatest lessons for living embodied in the world of sports. I'd like to share with you just a few of those ideals and principles, believing that they might help you as you fight and play the game of life, as you are competing and striving to win, as you are meeting problems and circumstances.

One of the great lessons I've learned in athletics is that you've got to discipline your life. No matter how good you may be, you've got to be willing to cut out of your life those things that keep you from going to the top.

In 1948 we were on board the SS *America*, going to London for the big world championships there. Dean Cromwell, our coach from Southern California, called together the 500 young men and women who made up the team. He said, "There is very little I can tell you about your specialty. You all know more about your event than I do, but there is one thing I can tell you as you go into these world championships. If you want to win, lay off smoking, drinking or anything of an incontinent nature that keeps you from doing your best."

I was startled to hear old Dean make that remark, but even more amazing to me was the fact that, out of the 500 young men and women on that team, I didn't see five people smoking and drinking during that entire trip. I saw grown men and women, veterans of World War II, twenty-six, twenty-seven, twenty-eight years of age. I saw them refuse to eat second helpings. I saw them refuse to go on sightseeing excursions. I saw them refuse to do anything but what was central in winning those Olympic championships. I saw boys go to bed at eight o'clock at night and get up at four o'clock in the morning. I saw them stay at the training base and train as often as three times a day. And I've become convinced, with that experience, that one of the great secrets for success in athletics is a clean and disciplined life.

I've come home from three Olympics convinced that one of the reasons why America does so well is because

American young men and women are disciplined in terms of cutting out of their lives those things that keep them from really going to the top. Is not this a great principle for all of living? The people who will really accomplish great things in life are those who are willing to discipline their lives, who maintain their health, their vitality, their efficiency through this process of rigorous discipline in what they take into their bodies and what they do in life. It's a very important thing, in terms of championship living.

There is another great principle in athletics. You've got to learn to work hard and to do plenty of it. Someone says, "Oh, you don't have to learn that in *athletics*. You can learn it in every realm of life." That's true. But there's a sense in which an athlete has either got to learn it or he just never accomplishes anything. I know this is contrary to the opinions of a lot of people. A lot of people have the idea that athletes are born, and not made, that athletes come into the world with a certain set of coordinated abilities or talents, that they step on a gridiron or a basketball court or a track or a golf course and just rely on this natural coordination.

I have hobnobbed with a few champions, and I'm convinced that hard work is far more important than natural ability. I was on a national team a few years back with a fellow named Herb McKenley. In 1947 Herb astounded the world by establishing a new world's record in the quarter mile, running it in 46.3. And when Herb did that, newspaper writers and radio commentators began saying, "Here's a natural athlete; here's a born runner!" The implication was that all Herb had to do was to go out there and move along on the track, and a world's record was just bound to follow.

Well, that didn't quite jibe with my experience, because I noticed Herb was one of the first ones on the track and one of the last ones to leave it. One night after practice, when I was going home and Herb was coming in from the track, the last one in that night, I met him at the door; I tapped him on the back and I said, "Herb, I understand you're one of these natural boys, that you don't have to train like the rest of us. That doesn't quite square with the fact that you work harder than anybody else on this track."

Herb laughed and said, "That's the silliest thing I've ever read or heard of in my life. You know, the first time I ever tried to run as a boy in Jamaica, I fell down because I couldn't coordinate my knees with my feet. Ever since that day I've been running *continually*, and I attribute that world's record to ten years of hard work." I was glad to hear him say that, because that had been my own experience.

But two years later, in a big meet in Madison Square Garden in New York, I saw Herb beaten by five or six fellows in a very poor time, and I couldn't figure out what had happened to him. I went up to him after the race and put my arm around him and asked, "What was the matter tonight, fellow? That was the worst race I've ever seen you run." He looked at me and said, "I'm not going to feed you a line. The truth of the matter is that I haven't been training as I know I ought to train. I feel that if I could get one good season under my belt, I could run the times that I used to run, but right now I can't do it because I'm out of shape. I just haven't been working as I know I should."

Herb was learning through bitter experience the lesson that every athlete will learn when he stops working. Stop working, and your power, your ability, your endurance, your form will leave you. There's only one way you can get to the top and stay there, in athletics, and that's through long hours of hard work. Many of you reading this may have unusual talent. You may have all the personal qualities necessary for success. You may have ability in art or music, or some great intellectual sensitivity or potentiality. But those talents will never flower and develop unless you are willing to pay the price of hard work. As the psychologists have put it, the most creative principle of personality development is "hard work and plenty of it." I've come to agree with Thomas A. Edison, America's great scientist, who said that "Genius is 1 percent inspiration and 99 percent perspiration." The secret of life is 99 percent perspiration. You can learn it in this world of sports, but you can apply it much quicker in other realms of human endeavor. It is work that carries a man to the top in any field.

Then there is another great quality. You've got to have faith and confidence in what you can do. I have never seen a real champion in my life who didn't have oozing out of him this quality of belief, or this conviction that he *could* do it—a will or a mental attitude that says, "I *know* I can do it." Many people have mistaken this for egotism. But as I've seen it in the lives of champions, I think they *believe* it, and because they turn this power of faith on their lives, it's amazing what they do. I've seen world's records broken before the contestants ever stepped out on the track. On the other hand, I've seen fellows hopelessly beaten before the gun went off. What beat them was not their physical ability but their mental attitude. They gave up before the race began.

As important as a body is in athletics, it is not as important as the frame of mind or the mental perspective that a fellow has. You can only go as high in life as you dare to believe you can go. Hitch your wagon to a star; aim for the great things in life. As Browning puts it: "But a man's reach should exceed his grasp, or what's a heaven for?" I dare to believe this: what a man thinks in his mind has a way of becoming reality in life. John Milton expressed it well when he said: "The mind is its own place, and in itself can make a heaven of hell, a hell of heaven." It's what you think that makes the difference.

Another great quality, one of the most important in an athlete's development, is the ability *to take defeat and to bounce back to victory*. I've seen fellows in all kinds of situations. I've seen them riding high, with flashbulbs in their faces, and their pictures in the newspapers, on a glory road of victory after victory, success after success. And then I've seen these boys beaten, and I've seen their power and their enthusiasm destroyed. I've seen great potential athletes, who had a great future, just quit and give up in defeat.

But I have never really seen a great champion who quit when he was beaten: he somehow has that quality of soul that refuses to go down; he bounces back to an even greater victory. In 1948 we were in the Dyche Stadium in Chicago for the Olympic trials. There was a boy there who was acclaimed as probably the finest Olympic prospect America had, a fellow by the name of Harrison Dillard, a wonderful athlete from Cleveland, Ohio. I happen to know Harrison personally. We have made a number of trips together, and have roomed together. I think he is one of the greatest athletes I have ever met. I saw Harrison as he got down to his mark in the 110-meter hurdles. He hadn't been beaten in eighty-three consecutive races. In two and a half years no one had come close to him. He was the prime hurdler of the world. They got down to their marks—six boys; of those six, only three could qualify for the Olympic team. They were out there giving everything they had. They got set. The gun went off. Harrison lunged out to an early lead. He was about a yard and a half ahead at the first hurdle. But somehow he overstrode and hit the second hurdle. He practically fell down on the third and stumbled and draped himself over the last hurdle.

I'll never forget it as long as I live. I was standing nearby and I saw Harry come up off that hurdle and look down the track. His lower jaw dropped, and that cold realization of defeat began to creep into his face, and I wondered if a fellow could ever feel worse. He had missed the Olympic teams, and an Olympic championship that was a cinch was gone because he couldn't even represent the United States. Could a fellow *ever* feel worse?

Harrison told me afterwards that right there, at that hurdle, looking down the track and watching those boys go on to claim his berth on the team, he made one of the greatest decisions of his running career. That was to come back and to change that defeat into victory. And so, a few moments later, he qualified for the 100 meters. He barely made the team for third place by nosing out Eddie Conwell *by a quarter of an inch.*

They went to London. No one gave this made-over hurdler a chance. But when they got down on their marks in

Wembley Stadium, one of them was a fellow who knew how to take defeat. When the gun went off before 100,000 people, he lunged out, dug in with everything he had, hit the tape in 10.3 to tie Jesse Owens's Olympic record. He had won the 100-meter championship, an event not his own, to claim probably the greatest championship of his life.

Four years later in Helsinki I saw him run his specialty, the hurdles, in 13.7 to win another Olympic championship. It's the sort of thing that makes champions. They don't quit when they're beaten. They bounce back to an even more glorious victory. They not only do it in competition; they do it in life.

Have you ever read the story of Glenn Cunningham, the story of a little boy who, at the age of five, had his legs so terribly burned by a fire in his home that the doctors claimed he would be a hopeless cripple the rest of his life? They said he would never be able to walk, that there was no hope for him. But they underestimated the heart and soul of little Glenn Cunningham. His mother tells of how she used to push back the curtain and look out the window and see Glenn as he would reach up and take hold of an old plow; with a hand on each handle he began to make those gnarled and twisted legs begin to function, and with every step a step of pain, Glenn Cunningham began to walk. And pretty soon he began to trot, and before long he was running. In 1934 he set a world mile record of 4:06.8. He'll go down in history as one of the great legendary runners of all time, having also run the mile in 4:04.4. It does not count officially, but at the time it was two seconds faster than the world's record and this was done by a boy who at the age of five faced one of the greatest defeats of life.

It's this that makes champions in competition, as in life; this ability to take defeat and change the very thing that spelled defeat into the very thing that makes champions.

You know as well as I do that life isn't all a bed of roses, that there are times when life is hard and cruel, when you meet heartache and setback and defeat. The real winner in life is the one who can meet them with a stiff upper lip, with a quality of soul that refuses to go down, with a faith in God, a courage that somehow enables him to keep on going. You can't beat a man or a woman who refuses to be beaten. They'll bounce back. They'll be triumphant.

One last thing that I've found in athletics: you've got to have something to inspire you. You've got to have something outside of you, a power greater than your own, that somehow comes into a tired body and aching muscles and just inspires you to go on to your very best. Now I know you're going to say that here's an old preacher trying to point up the spiritual side of life. Well, if I were the only athlete who ever called upon this power, you might be justified in thinking that. I'm not the only one, by a long shot. I wish I could tell you of conversations and experiences that I have had with these boys who, when they've given everything else they've got, call on God and find a power greater than their own to help them.

A lot of people have the idea it's like the boy who, when he hits the three-quarter mark and his legs are tired, looks up to heaven and says, "O God, you pick them up and I'll put them down." Well, it isn't *that* sort of an attitude that I sense in these champions. They have a way of finding something deep down within them, an untapped resource or a power that lies dormant in every man and woman.

And when they have given everything else, they call on this power.

At the Millrose Games in 1948 in Madison Square Garden in New York, I saw a boy come pounding around the track, lap after lap, until, when he hit the three-quarter mark in the mile, his time was 3:03.1. It looked like a new world's record. The crowd began to cheer, but this boy, Gil Dodds, was in trouble; his legs were beginning to wobble, he was grimacing with pain and gasping for air. But as he was going around the curve I saw him lift up his eyes and pray. And I saw those wobbly legs begin to straighten up. The frown on his face turned to a smile and he began to sprint. He hit the tape in 4:05.3, a new world's indoor record. When the crowd finally quieted down, they had Gil say a word over the loudspeaker; he simply grabbed the mike and said into it, "I want to praise the Lord for helping me run tonight." On the train going back to Chicago I said to him, "Gil, what did you pray for at that three-quarter mark?" He said, "I simply said to the Lord, 'Lord, I've come this far on my own strength. With Your help and Your power I know I can go the rest of the way.' I felt the surge of that divine power within me, and it helped me to that tape."

Some time ago in Sweden, I talked to Gunder Hagg, the boy who once held more world's records than any other runner alive, voted the outstanding runner of the century. He told me, as we talked in his sports shop, that he had never broken a record without, before and during the race, praying and finding a spiritual strength that helped him win.

I talked to Dutch Warmerdam, the boy who holds the world's record in the pole vault. He said, "Bob, I've never cleared a height over 15 feet without asking God to help me, and I know He has." I've talked to one fellow after another, fellows like Parry O'Brien, Bob McMillan, other boys in the world of track and field, all-American basketball players, all-American football players like Don Moomaw and others, who all say that they call on God for strength.

There's a power in which you live and move and have your being, and if you'll call on that power, it will help you accomplish the great things and the good things of life.

If you'll work hard, if you'll have faith, if you'll learn to take defeat and come back, if you rely on the power of God, you'll be triumphant in the game of life—you'll be a champion in the greatest endeavor of all.

# AIMING FOR THE TOP

The essence of what I have to say in this chapter grows out of an experience that I had in Toronto, Canada. I was invited to participate in a pole-vaulting exhibition, and while I was there, I had the opportunity to observe one of the most fantastic sports accomplishments that I have ever seen. George Duthie, the sports director of Canada, asked me if I would like to watch sixteen men and women try to swim Lake Ontario. Part of the Canadian exhibition was a challenge to the youth of Canada to see if any one of them could swim Lake Ontario. Now this lake is 39.5 miles across at its narrowest point and the temperature of the water, at this particular time, was 50°. Because of the inclement weather, they almost postponed the swim; it seemed impossible. However, at the insistence of the swimmers, they finally went ahead with the plans. I was in the back of a boat and watched the contestants plunge into the cold Ontario water and begin to stroke their way out across the lake. At one, two, and three miles, many of them dropped out. Some of them kept on swimming for seven or eight miles, until their lips were blue and cold and their whole bodies were numb. Gradually all of them quit except for one lone swimmer by the name of Clifford Lungsen. Somehow this big barrel-chested fellow kept reaching out, stroking his way through the water. He reached the halfway mark, the coldest point, and kept right on swimming. His sweetheart happened to be in the back of our boat, and she kept urging him on, giving him encouragement. As I sat there watching this boy numb with cold, fighting his way along almost oblivious of pain, I asked myself why men try to do such impossible things. I watched him as, again and again, he resisted being taken out and went on swimming. To make a long story short, he made it to the other side. He touched his hand down on the shore over on the Toronto side, and as the roar of 10,000 people greeted him, he stood up to acknowledge the ovation. As he tried to lift his hand, however, he collapsed into the arms of two doctors. He received treatment for two weeks. Again and again the thought has gone through my mind: why do men try to do such impossible things?

I've seen the same spirit in the world of track and field where you watch the boy during the mile race as he comes off the track after three and three-quarter laps. You watch him as he perspires all over, as he gasps for air; you watch him struggling through fatigue, and you see him as he picks up his knees and drives with all he's got down the straightaway, into the tape. Why? Because he wants to break four minutes in the mile. He will run down to the very nub in order to accomplish this. As I have watched many and many a boy strive for it, and some of them do it, the same question presents itself: why do they keep aiming for the top, taxing their bodies, minds and spirits to the ultimate?

I saw it in a motion picture not long ago. Seated very comfortably in my living-room chair, I watched the dramatic portrayal of five men trying to climb one of the most difficult mountains in the world. They went through frigid cold, hanging precariously between life and death again and again, their bodies almost going out into oblivion. I saw those men as they hung on desperately, as a team, inching their way up the ice and snow until they stood out supreme on the top of that mountain. All through the movie the thought went through my mind: *Why do men try to accomplish the impossible, risking life and limb itself in order to attain the peaks?* I have come to believe that the answer lies in the fact that man is endowed with an instinctive impulse to get to the top; that when the sports world is analyzed, it can only be explained in terms of men who have a peculiar psychology of wanting to break records, to do the impossible, to accomplish what has never been accomplished before. This spirit is not only evident in the sports world; it may be found in every realm of life. For example, no matter how good a man's business is, he wants to make it bigger and better, to attain something even beyond profit, to do something with it nobody else has done. Many people tell me that the only reason business-men work is for money. I don't believe it. I think many of them are trying to accomplish something tremendous with their lives. The same is true in the world of science, where no matter how great the discovery, or how tremendous the ideas that have been uncovered in the past decade, the scientific mind keeps reaching out, grasping for new ideas in a continuing search for new truths. A musician wants each composition to excel over the last, and the artist, no matter how great his painting might be, keeps rubbing out the canvas until he has caught what his mind's eye wants to convey.

In the spiritual world, the apostle Paul expressed it beautifully when he said: "Forgetting what lies behind and looking to the future, I press on toward the mark of the high calling of God in Christ Jesus my Lord" (see Phil. 3:13–14). Here was one of the greatest men, outside of Christ, who ever lived. And yet, you see, he was still reaching out. In spite of all he had accomplished, he had higher goals, higher marks that he was striving for. Deep in the heart of every person are great goals that he wants to accomplish. In some people it is a burning desire, an obsession, while in others it may be a faintly felt thing. But it is in every human being. No matter how much man may accomplish, he will always be frustrated. No matter how much you gain in the way of wealth, no matter how much you achieve in the way of athletic greatness or in scientific progress, there will still be that gnawing within you, that sense of not having done enough. Man cannot be content, because if he is—progress stops. This frustration is the indispensable prerequisite of progress; for as long as a man can refuse to be content with his efforts, as long as he keeps having goals beyond those he has already attained, he will be carried on to greater achievements. The Olympic slogan, three words in Latin meaning "higher, longer, faster," expresses it beautifully.

These words written on every Olympic stadium in the world portray the spirit of man: no matter how high he has gone he wants to go higher, no matter how much distance he has traversed he wants to go longer, no matter how fast he has run a race he wants to run it faster.

Sometimes men forget that there are certain qualities of life that are indispensable to those who would reach the top. It's not enough to sit by idly gazing at the mountain peaks one would climb; it is not enough to look across a great expanse of lake and wish one could swim it. It's not enough to watch men run the mile in four minutes and wish for the same strength.

The first indispensable quality is *self-control*. If I have learned one thing in sports, it is that before a man ever scales the heights of greatness without, he must first of all learn to control himself within. Most of the great champions of the world learn to hold their emotions in check; they have a certain amount of emotional stability. On the other hand, I have seen some potentially great athletes miss their goals, miss reaching the top, because they couldn't control themselves. I think of one athlete I knew who was endowed with a tremendous body, 6 feet 4 inches tall, 195 pounds, supple and well coordinated. He could run the 100 yards in 9.8, he could broad jump 25 feet, he could run the hurdles in 14 flat and he starred in football and basketball. There wasn't anything he couldn't do—he was "a natural," if there ever was one. But while he had this tremendous physical development, he lacked one very important mental trait: *he couldn't control his temper*. I have seen this boy in competition after competition, way out ahead of everyone, his splendid body working for him, when all of a sudden he would raise a crossbar, wobble a discus throw and then—as we say in track and field—he would blow his top. He would argue with the officials, quarrel with his competitors and—which is worse—fight with himself. Whenever that happened, he was helpless; he just went to pieces. He could have been great; he wasn't.

Michigan State played UCLA in the Rose Bowl in 1956. It was a thrilling game. Actually I was pulling for UCLA, because the late Red Saunders, the coach at UCLA, had asked me to come out and speak to the Bruins. After speaking with them, I realized that many of them were deeply religious. It was a wonderful thing to hear a big fellow like Jim Decker say, "The Lord has been good to me this year." Or to hear Bob Davenport, the UCLA all-American full-back, say, "I've had a divine coach, in my career." As a ninth-grade boy, Bob's knees had been so badly hurt in football that he seemed destined never to play big-time football, but the divine coach had brought him through. Naturally, I was pulling for those boys as I had seldom pulled for a team before. Michigan State was the superior team; there was no question about that. They had had greater competition in the past season. But UCLA played over their heads, played them to a standstill, while 102,000 people went wild. The score near the end of the game, with only one minute left to play, was 14 to 14. It looked like a great moral victory for UCLA. They got the ball on the 50-yard line, and in that minute they could have won the game, but something happened in the huddle. Seven or eight fellows began to call the signals, there were arguments, confusion, and they were penalized for taking too much time. Then the coach called a play from the sidelines, and they were penalized again. From deep in their own territory they had to kick. During the last seven seconds of the game, with Michigan State in charge of the ball, a young sophomore from Michigan State tried a field goal. He swung his leg through, and with perfect control and mastery of his emotions, he kicked that ball squarely and through the uprights of the goal—and in the stands, about fifty Michigan State fans landed on top of me. It was one of the most jubilant expressions of victory I have ever seen.

Some people will say that the game was won by the toot of the whistle, that the penalties decided the game. But I believe that the determining factor in the game was self-control. Boys jumping offside, arguing in the huddle and delaying the game—these things, while they may seem small, cost big and important games. I wonder how many games have been lost this way?

I always think of self-control when I watch a hammer-thrower. A big 200-pounder will take a 16-pound ball and whirl it around his head three times, twirling like a top, lean back at 45° and let the hammer go with a terrific grunt. But I have watched these fellows sometimes lose control of the hammer, misplace their feet for just a fraction of a second—and literally throw themselves out of the ring. As a matter of fact, I have seen some of them go farther than the hammer! I wonder if that isn't a symbol of life; our emotions, our wills, the dynamic force within us is that whirling hammer, and if we lose control of it for a split second, it can literally throw us. The great question in life is: Am I going to throw it or is it going to throw me? This is what men must learn. The apostle Paul was talking good sense when he said, "Everyone who competes in the games exercises self-control in all things. They then do it to receive a perishable wreath, but we an imperishable" (1 Cor. 9:25 NASB). If you want to be great in sports, you've got to learn to control your emotions. And it is so in all of life.

Secondly, you must use your mind. Now this may sound strange, because in the sports world, too often we think that any man seven feet tall makes a great basketball player, and that 250 pounds of man makes a good football player. But I have found in this sports world that there is a lot more to it than the body, that at least 50 percent of success depends on the mind: what you think, your goals, your faith, your determination, and the creative imagination of your mind.

I remember talking to Hamp Poole when he was coach of the Los Angeles Rams. He took me up to his office, after I had had the privilege of talking to the Rams. I was amazed. There were stacks of typewriter paper all over his desk, and on every one of these papers was a play, a diagram. When I said that football was getting to be a science, he replied, "Most people don't realize it, but football is more a game of thinking than anything else." He told me of plays where the quarterback would go back, count up to a certain number, whirl and throw to a spot where the halfback or the end had to be, or the play didn't go. He told me of offensive and defensive maneuvers in which the guards and tackles had to go across the line at a precise second or the play collapsed. He said, "Everything depends upon split-second timing—a man has to be alert and thinking all the time."

In the field of pro football, I think of Doak Walker, one of my close friends, who only weighs 170 pounds, and stands 5 feet 9½ inches tall—but he is the first boy ever to make all-American three times. He once told me, "I have been able to play big-time football for just one reason: I try to outthink the other fellow. When I am off the field, I am watching defensive maneuvers, trying to find a crack in the defense. When I go into the game again, I am still trying to outthink that one man. As I run with the ball, I try to think whether I can dodge him; I try to use my blockers to the best advantage. If there has been any success in my running with the ball, it has been because I have had such fine blockers—fellows who think with me as we move down the field."

In the world of track and field that I know so well, I have seen this ability to think come through again and again. I remember a good friend of mine named Bud Held, a javelin-thrower on the Olympic team in 1952. Bud had what was, at that time, the finest javelin in the world, and he could throw about 230 feet. One day, after a couple of bad throws, he said, "These javelins just aren't any good." I laughed at him, thinking he was just looking for an alibi. After one particularly poor throw of about 235 feet, he said that he could make a better javelin than that himself. Some of the fellows who heard it scoffed and laughed a bit. But Bud has a master's degree in engineering, and he went home to his basement workshop and began making a *hollow* javelin. The first time he tried it out was in Pasadena, California. I happened to be there, and so were some sports writers who had heard about it. Bud blazed down the runway, planted his feet, let it go—and the thing went straight up in the air, going about 75 feet. There was much mockery and laughter but about two months later, in Pasadena with a smaller group, Bud went down the runway, planted his feet, bent in and let his javelin go—and it went out 263 feet and 10 inches to break by five feet the old world's record that had stood for fifteen years. You may say that Bud had a terrific arm—but more than that, he had used his mind to break that record. Today, the hollow javelin is used all over the world. It has revolutionized javelin throwing, and records are going out, out, out.

Every advance in track and field has been coupled with some man using his mind. I remember it was claimed that a man couldn't jump any higher than 6 feet, 6 inches; that was the ultimate. There just wasn't enough spring in the human body to exceed that height. Harold Osborn, one of my good friends back at the University of Illinois, won the Olympic decathlon and the Olympic high jump and held the world's record in the high jump at one time. He was told, because he was 5 feet 10 inches tall, that he couldn't possibly jump over 6 feet 6. But Harold developed a new technique and jumped almost 6 feet 10.

When Parry O'Brien, the shot-putter, was a junior at Southern California, he was throwing the shot 54 or 55 feet. One day, while Parry was watching a boy put the shot in the old, conventional way, he got an idea. Maybe he could twist his body around a little bit and get down a little lower, hit the shot all the way from the ground, and perhaps he could get it farther. He tried again and again and couldn't improve much on his old form, but he kept working on it. At first the fellows scoffed and mocked him. People never want to accept the new; they want to cling to the old. That's the way the reactionary mind works. In clinging to the old, many great minds have been lost to the progress of the world. Parry began to put the shot, crouching lower and lower in the ring, and little by little it worked better. It went out to 57 feet, 58 feet, 59 feet. Then one day he threw it over 60 feet, 61 feet 10, 62 feet 5, then 63 feet 2. Parry O'Brien has revolutionized shot putting. All over the world they are using "the Parry O'Brien style."

Do you see what I mean when I say that *the mind is involved*? In music, art, the world of the intellect, science, business, in the home, in religion, in our communities, there are tremendous things that have still to be done. And these things will only be done if we stop thinking that the only way is the old way. We've got to use our creative imaginations. We've got to think! Someone has said that every problem that man has could be solved if only man would think. George Washington Carver was born on a plantation and didn't have much of a formal education, but he went out every day and talked with the flowers; he would hold up a peanut in his hand and say, "O God, what's in a peanut?" He developed some 250 products out of peanuts and some 200 products out of the petals of flowers, proving himself to be one of the most creative scientists America has ever produced. Or think of a Benjamin Franklin, tying a key to the tail of a kite. Nobody knew about electricity until Franklin did that. This is what has made America great: creative thinking! I believe the whole idea of American democracy rests upon it. I think the future of the world rests upon it—upon the creative thinking of the individual in his work and his worship and his play.

Thirdly, you just can't be discouraged. Now I know this may sound trite, but in the sports world you come up against it every day. How many great champions, at one time or another, have been discouraged? I have never talked to a champion who hasn't told me that at one time he was ready to give up, that he had reached a point where he just couldn't see his way out, and in disappointment and disillusionment he was just about to quit—when suddenly he reasserted his faith in himself and in what he could do and went on to accomplish some great thing.

With this in mind, I think of the greatest baseball player who has ever lived. Some of you may disagree with me as to who that baseball player is, but I think of a boy who wasn't a natural, who had to do everything the hard way. As a boy he was fat and awkward—he just couldn't seem to do things the easy way; he made error upon error. The story goes that, as a bungling kid, he made an error and the winning run was scored against his team. One of his teammates came up to him, threw his glove down in front of him and said, "For heaven's sake, why don't you quit? You're always ruining our team!" The boy looked up and said, "I know I have made mistakes, but I am going to make one less mistake every day and I am going to accomplish something in baseball." This boy, tempted to give up in that minute of discouragement, worked after hours. He began to practice his swing until he could hit the ball. He worked at first base until he could make the plays—and to make the story short, that wobbly, awkward kid hardened down to rock. He made the New York Yankee baseball team, he played 2,130 consecutive ball games for the greatest record in baseball. He tied the great Babe Ruth in home runs in one year. He had a lifetime batting average of well over .300. I think in terms of spirit, attitude and determination he was the greatest baseball player in history. His name was Lou Gehrig. When you are discouraged, use Gehrig's philosophy and start by saying this, "I am going to make one less mistake per day!"

Have you heard the story of Charlie Boswell, the all-American halfback from the University of Alabama and a baseball star as well? Charlie was offered professional contracts in both football and baseball. In World War II he answered the call of his country. In a maneuver in Europe, a shell hit his tank; in helping others to get out of the burning death trap, he delayed his own exit a little too long, and another shell hit them. In the explosion that followed, Charlie Boswell's body was hurled 50 feet. He was left lying there, burned and broken. They finally found him and removed him to a hospital; one week later he regained consciousness and, to his horror, found that he was totally blind. How would you like to meet discouragement like that? Boswell, the all-around athlete, 205 pounds of muscle, found it hard. He stumbled and fell over his cane, broke it and almost quit; but with his wife encouraging him and breathing a prayer for God to help him, he went on. One day, in a rehabilitation hospital, a friend came up to him and asked him if he would like to take up golf. Charlie said, "Gee, I'd love to, but I can't see. How in the world can I hit a golf ball when I can't even see it?" The friend told him that he would help him. He took Charlie Boswell out on the golf course, put a golf club in his hand and made him swing at a ball that he had never seen before. The first time Charlie hit it, he drove it 200 yards down the middle. He found himself in the swing and started training and practicing. Totally blind, he won the world championship for blind golfers, and on his home course in Birmingham, Alabama, he shot 38 for 9 holes. Can you imagine this? I go out on the golf course and I can see everything there is on the whole course (and that's where I generally am—all over the whole course), but I think a lot of this man without eyes, in a game requiring depth perception and vision, shooting almost par. It's an incredible thing, but it proves what can happen when a man refuses to be discouraged. I don't believe anyone ever got to the top without going through the valleys. Like the mountain climbers reaching out for the peak, they have to go down before they can go up. The spirit of man sometimes falls into moods of depression and doubt, but if you can fight your way out of it and keep on going, with your mind fixed on the top and making one less mistake per day and swinging away and doing the best you can, then you've got the secret of going to the top.

Lastly, you've got to really aim for the top. I have known many athletes who limited themselves by the failure to comprehend what they really could do. Oh, they had a little goal, or some small thing that they wanted to accomplish, but it wasn't really big enough to challenge them, nor great enough to pull out the deepest within them. I have seen athletes with enormous potential drifting along when they could be great—and all of a sudden, someone would lift their mental horizons with a vision of what they could *really* do. I have seen men with such vision do the fantastic, whittling tenths of seconds off world's records. It's amazing what can happen when you really aim for the top, really reach out for the thing with all you've got.

A good friend of mine is Don Bragg, a pole vaulter. I remember him when he was jumping about 14 feet. He couldn't seem to go much higher. He was 6 feet 3 inches tall, weighed 195 pounds and had huge arms. As a kid, he used to play Tarzan, climbing the trees around his home; he had built up arms that are about 16 or 17 inches in the biceps. He was as strong as an ox. I looked at him, and I couldn't understand why he couldn't jump any higher. That fast, and that big and that strong, he ought to jump about 16 feet. I couldn't figure it out. But one day in Philadelphia we were competing against each other and I walked up to get some tape from Don Bragg; and I noticed that on the bag that held his pole for the pole vault—a 16-foot-long bag—were written the words, "The world's record, 15 feet 9 inches, or bust"; he had his name written under it. I looked at the thing and trembled a little. Then Don came up and said, "Bob, some time I want you to baptize me." I was startled. I could see a whole new seriousness of purpose coming up in this boy. I said, "Sure, I'd love to do it, Don," and went on down the runway, trembling as I thought, *Great guns, if that 6 feet 3 inches, 200 pounds ever gets religion, I'm through!* Don had set his sights on something higher; he would never be content now with 14 feet. He made 14 feet 6, he made 15 feet, he made 15 feet 3, he made 15 feet 5, and barely missed the world's record of 15 feet, 9 inches.

This is what happens when men lift their mental horizons. You never know what potential you've got within you until you reach out for the highest. You never know what you've got until you get something that pulls out everything within you.

I think of a race between John Landy and Jim Bailey. Landy had come to town as one of the very few sub-four-minute milers, and a huge crowd came out to the Los

Angeles Coliseum to see him run. Running against him was Jim Bailey, an unknown from Oregon University, a fellow countryman of Landy. Landy took off at a very fast pace; his first three-quarters time was only 3:01.5. He was on the way to run the mile under four minutes. Back in third spot was Jim Bailey, about ten yards behind. All of a sudden Bailey got an idea: "Maybe I can push John to a new world's record." He began to reach out, pumping his legs as he never had before; he closed the gap on Landy and as they hit the backstretch, he was only about five yards behind. Then he got another idea: "Maybe I can *tie* John Landy!" Blazing down the backstretch, he caught him, and in the middle of the curve, with about 100 yards left to go, another idea hit him: "Maybe I can *beat* John Landy." Running with muscle and mental faith that he never had before, Bailey moved out and went by Landy, drove into the tape to win in the greatest performance of his life—3:58.6—and experts believe that he could have run 3:56 if he had only thought about it earlier. But the fantastic thing about this story is that until this time, Jim Bailey hadn't run a mile in under 4:05.6; he just couldn't seem to get below that. It wasn't until this race, when a champion set the standard high for him, that Jim Bailey began to think in terms of something better than 4:05.6; then he accomplished the great feat of his career. This is what happens when men reach out, when they aim for the top, when they really go for it.

We must aim for the top not only in terms of athletic records but also in terms of character. As I think of this, I think again of Landy, of the boy who was beaten, who back in Australia before coming to the U.S. had trained for two months for the Australian championships. This was in

Melbourne; 50,000 people came out to watch John Landy because it looked as if he was going to break his own world's record of 3:58. He took off; the first lap was tremendous, and at the end of the half Landy was running strongly. The roar of the crowd greeted him as he blazed around the curve. A smile broke across his face and he *knew* this was it; he raced down the backstretch at a sensational pace, but as he did so a young high school boy running against him stumbled and fell, and John Landy, without thinking, stopped, reached down and pulled the boy up. To the consternation of the crowd he stood there until he found that the boy was all right; then at the urging of the boy, he went on. The others had gone on beyond him, but Landy caught them and went into the tape in 4:04.2. Experts say that his time would have been 3:59, or under, if he had not stopped. Do you get the point? Here was a man for whom stopping to help a fallen runner was more important than a national championship. When the greatest sports stories are written, they won't forget the story of the boy for whom character meant more than fame.

This is what I mean by aiming for the top. You must aim for the highest there is in the universe; you must aim not only at character, you must aim for God. This may shock you, but some of the greatest athletes I have ever known have been athletes who have aimed for what they considered the greatest thing in the universe—namely, God. I think of a boy who has been drifting along, then all of a sudden finds God: I think of Rafer Johnson and the inspiration that it gives him. I think of my own life, where it took aiming for God to really pull out the deepest within me, in the sports world. I think of Bud Wilkinson, the great coach at Oklahoma University, who has perhaps the greatest record in modern football; he wrote these words in a sports magazine, "You show me a boy who has a spiritual quality and I will show you a boy who will make a great football player. There is a relationship between the spiritual and the physical." I agree with Bud Wilkinson; it isn't until a man does that, until he reaches out for the greatest dimension, that he accomplishes his best. Doak Walker once told me that he never went on a field without a prayer. Otto Graham told me that he always asks God for help. When men reach out for God, they do their best. Jesus put it this way: "Seek ye first the kingdom of God . . . and all these [other] things shall be added unto you" (Matt. 6:33). Put the highest thing in the universe at the center of your mind and—it's odd, but everything else begins to come to life around you. This is what I have found in the sports world: that men want to go to the top, that men embody within themselves the qualities that make the top obtainable; they have self-control and they rigorously control themselves. They use their minds, their creative imaginations; they are never discouraged, they keep looking for the peak and they aim for the highest. They go for the ultimate, they want the deepest there is, and many of them aim for God. Well, this, for me, is the top; and I hope and I pray that every person who reads this will set his goals a little higher and reach out for the truly greatest in life.

# Being the Person
# I Ought to Be

Each and every one of us has some sort of goal or
ideal or objective as to the kind of person that we
would like to be. But the great tragedy with most of
us is this: We don't know how to be the person we ought
to be. We have goals, but they are more or less vague abstractions, nebulous. They might even be clearly defined,
but because we don't know how to accomplish our goals,
they go begging, and we never arrive at being the kind of
person we want to be.

Now, what we need is a method, a technique, a means to
help us accomplish our goal. And this is exactly where the
sports world lives for me. The sports world has a unique
authority in this respect: it not only has goals, victories,
triumphs that it strives for, but it provides vivid illustrations
of *how* these goals may be reached. In fact, the sports world

is absolutely set up so that it deals with the means, with the techniques of arriving at the goals. Many preachers and teachers point out what people ought to be, but they don't really show them how.

Mankind does not want for ideals—in fact there has never been a time when ideals were so clearly formulated. People want to be great, they want to be successful, they want to accomplish great things, but the tragedy is that they stress *what* they want to be so much that they forget the "how," the technique. Now the sports world is a concrete world, dealing not with abstractions but with living, vital flesh and blood. You don't just talk a big one in the locker room. You've got to go out on the field and sweat, you've got to go out on the field and hurt, and take the bruises, the bumps. The sports world lives in this kind of thing for men.

The sports world is a realistic world of tough competition. There is always another line to go through, obstacles and difficulties to be overcome, distances to be traversed. It is no dream world, but a world of physical performance where an ideal must be translated into a chin-up, a push-up, a run, a tackle, a block. This is the opinion Plato expressed in *The Republic* when he said that every child should have athletic experience—he called it gymnastics—because he felt that a man could not reason correctly nor engage in the higher functions of life unless he had a toughening of the spirit that athletics provided. I agree. I think that there are vital lessons, dealing with common everyday experiences, to be learned on the athletic field and that they can't be learned in any other place.

In the matter of being the kind of person we ought to be, there is one very important means that the sports world recognizes: *You've got to analyze yourself, recognize your weaknesses and work on them.* Now this is one of the hardest things for a person to do. It is very easy for us to take a negative attitude toward our weaknesses, justifying them by saying that after all, we were born with this particular weakness—or we have just acquired it through the circumstances of life—and actually there is nothing we can do about it. Or we can defend a weakness, and in the process of this defense, we may start to build our lives around it, making the weakness the center of our lives instead of conquering the thing and overcoming it. Now you can't react negatively to your weaknesses like this and expect to attain success. Here again the glory of the sports world for me is that it deals with the overcoming of weaknesses. In fact, some of the greatest stories I know of are stories where men have recognized their weaknesses, dealt positively with them, overcome them and gone on to tremendous heights.

To me one of the greatest of these is a story about Rocky Marciano. I don't know what you think about boxing, but to me, the account of this boy who rose from practically nothing in the sports world to become the heavyweight champion of the world is one of the most thrilling stories in competitive sports. I agree with Gene Tunney when he says that no sport so symbolizes life in the raw as boxing. When Rocky first started boxing, he had one glaring weakness: He could barely hold his arms up. They were big arms, short and powerful—but the tragedy was that whenever he would go into the ring, after a couple of rounds his arms would get weary and would begin to descend slowly to his sides, and then of course, he would take a terrific beating from his sparring partners. Experts who saw Rocky Marciano said that, because of this one basic weakness, plus a lack of finesse and polish, he would never be great in the ring. Rocky, instead of quitting, developed an ingenious method of working on his weakness. He used to go down to a local swimming pool, submerge himself and flail his arms as hard as he could against the water. He would swing them against the buoyancy of the water for hours, forcing the arm muscles to develop against abnormal difficulties. This is the story of a man who became the undefeated heavyweight champion of the world simply because he worked on a weakness, and made out of that weakness a strength that carried him to boxing's greatest glory. This can happen when a person meets a weakness head-on, when he does something about it.

I think also, in this connection, of Bill Nieder, the shot-putter. He was a big, powerful fellow, playing football at the University of Kansas and slated for all-American. But one Saturday afternoon in a big ball game, he took a bone-crushing block across the knee and was crippled severely. Operation after operation proved unsuccessful and Bill was told that, because of his stiff right leg, he was through with sports, that he would never be able to compete again. Now many people would have taken refuge in a weakness like this. Bill could have made excuses. But one day, watching field and track men running and throwing the shot and discus, he decided that he would like to go out and throw the shot. As he threw the shot by the hour, trying to find an outlet for his pent-up energies, the knee began to bend, the exercise accomplishing what the doctors thought was impossible. The knee began to flex a little bit more each day.

The amazing part of this story is that eventually, through constant practice, he threw 62 feet, 2 inches to beat Parry O'Brien, the world's greatest shot-putter. He is one of the very few men who have thrown over 60 feet in the shot—and his chief power came from his right leg—the leg his doctors thought would be stiff and weak for the rest of his life.

Swimmer Keith Forbes provides another dramatic illustration out of the world of sports as to what can happen when a man faces his weakness positively, and changes it into the strength of his life. Few people know that when he was just a boy, playing cowboys and Indians, he took a wild leap, landed on a rock and crushed his hip in the process. One day Keith was swimming with the other boys in the YMCA and the coach noticed that, although he couldn't kick normally, he had a rather unusual ability to stroke his way through the water. He began to work with him, and Forbes developed a powerful stroke that compensated for his weakness. Keith Forbes went on to set about four American records and was third in the Olympic Games in 1948, beaten out by only half a yard by some of the finest specimens of physical power in the world. He has now become a doctor, specializing in work with crippled children. When you think of a Keith Forbes giving his life to this, you can see how a weakness may be turned into strength.

It happens often in life. Have you noticed that alcoholics, out of their former weakness, are often most effective in helping other men suffering from the same weakness? Many psychiatrists, I am told, have conquered in others the same emotional difficulties that they once conquered in themselves. Some of our greatest doctors specialize in diseases they once had themselves. These are vivid illustrations of what can happen when a man does something about his own weakness. I think this is what the Bible means when it says, "My strength is made perfect in weakness" (2 Cor. 12:9). I think God is telling us here that He won't help us justify our weaknesses, that He will not help us defend them, but that He will help us to turn them into strength. If you want to be great in any realm of life, analyze yourself, recognize your weaknesses and work on them.

Again, if you want to be the person you ought to be, *you've got to welcome competition*. This is a hard thing to do because there is a tendency within us to want to level off, to accept a certain standard as being "good enough." Now I know that the idea of competition is being criticized today by many leading educators who question its value. But may I simply assert this fact: You cannot escape competition in life. From the time a child is born until he dies, he is facing competition of one kind or another. It cannot be avoided; it is indispensable to progress. Now what do I mean by competition? Competition is someone setting a standard for you that you ought to set for yourself; it is that outside stimulus or impetus that forces you to set your own standards higher and to achieve a little higher mark. I have noticed another thing about competition: It pulls out the best there is in a man and the best in those around him. I remember when Parry O'Brien first put the shot 60 feet when the experts said it was absolutely impossible, that within four years' time, five men had thrown the shot over 60 feet.

I remember when they were talking about the four-minute mile. There were experts who thought that it was impossible for a human being to run a four-minute mile. Well, Roger Bannister ran the mile in 3:59.4 and within a couple of years, ten men had broken the four-minute record. On a track in Ireland, four men broke the world's record, which was 3:58, five finished under four minutes. Five men running the mile under four minutes in the same race! This gives you an idea of what competition does.

I shall never forget a race I saw in Mexico City during the Pan-American Games in 1955. Three boys went down to the mark in the 400-meter dash. Now if you had known these boys, you would have felt, as the American track team felt, that this was really going to be one of those races where all three men would run all out. The three men in the race were Jimmy Lea of the University of Southern California, Lou Jones from the East, and J. W. Mashburn of the Oklahoma A. and M. Whenever these three fellows met, it was a race down to the wire. None of them would yield an inch, not one would give in—they ran until they were simply exhausted. They lined up for the finals of the 400 meters—if you have ever tried to run in an altitude of 7,500 feet on a hot day, you know what these boys had in store—and when the gun went off, they took off at a sprint, arms pumping, legs driving; they went around the curve and down the backstretch, hitting the first 200 meters in under 22 seconds. That's really moving! You would have thought that under such conditions they would have let up, but they didn't. At the end of the first 200, they kept right on pumping—around the curve and into the straightaway with 40,000 people roaring. They were simply weak from exhaustion, Jimmy Lea driving all he had, his chin buried in his chest, Lou Jones with teeth gritted, maintaining the pace, and J. W. Mashburn, knees pumping like mad, mouth open a little but elbows pumping. They stayed right in there together, drove down the straightaway—and Lou Jones lunged out in the end, nipping the other two boys in a world's record time of 45.4. They collapsed on the track and had to have oxygen administered to them for 45 minutes before they were able to stand up again. Lou Jones told me afterwards, "Bob, I would never have accomplished that mark if it hadn't been for the other two boys." There were those who said that it was a freak time, so the same three boys hooked up in the Olympic tryouts in 1956 and the same thing happened. Lou Jones was on the outside, J. W. Mashburn and Jimmy Lea were there as was Charlie Jenkins. When the crack of the gun sounded, they took off and roared down the backstretch together. Lou Jones, knowing he was going to have to run the greatest race of his life to qualify for the Olympic team, broke out of the turn, sprinted down the straightaway and into the tape in 45.2. Afterwards, he told me once again, "Bob, I owe this record to J. W. Mashburn, Jimmy Lea and Charlie Jenkins, because they pulled out the best within me. I had to do it in order to beat them." I think Lou Jones was basically correct in recognizing the tremendous value of his competition.

I remember when I was in a small college in the East, Bridgewater College, and I pole-vaulted 12 feet, 6 inches to set a new Mason-Dixon Conference record. It was an amazing thing, according to them. I was eulogized and praised, and I thought that I was the cock of the walk at 12 feet, 6 inches. But I transferred and went to the University of Illinois. At that particular time, the University of Illinois had a terrific track team with a number of outstanding people from all over the world, including Herb McKenley, Billy Mathis, George Walker, Bob Reyberg and others. I'll never forget walking out on the track and swaggering up to the pole-vaulting pit with my pole in my hand—I was going to show these boys at the University of Illinois how to pole vault. Well, I laid my pole down, just waiting for an opportune moment to display my skill, when right in front of me, in a matter of 45 seconds, three boys roared down the runway and pole-vaulted 13 feet, 6 inches. Talk about a person being quickly humbled—my ego went out the bottom of my toes and if I could have crawled away from that place I would have, gladly. But the more I think about it the more I am convinced that that moment made me. I had to lift my horizons quickly. I had to force myself to realize that 12 feet 6 wasn't good enough, that if I was even going to make that team, I had to put out everything I had. Consequently, I began climbing rope as I have never climbed before. I did chin-ups, push-ups, I lifted weights, I worked every night, jumping 35 to 40 times, doing wind sprints. The more I think about it, those three boys brought out the best within me in that moment of competition. They helped me to accomplish the later heights of 15 feet and above because they made me lift my mental horizons. Competition forces you to re-evaluate your own ability, to set your standards higher, to lift your horizons so that you can accomplish greater things. It is amazing how this thing works. I have seen it happen in the Olympics time after time. Fellows will be drifting along, giving relatively mediocre performances, when they suddenly run up against the stiff competition found in the Olympic trials. Many world's records and American records fall during Olympic tryouts because the fellows realize that only one, two or three are selected for the Olympic team; they have to place in the first three or they just don't go!

In the 1956 Olympic tryouts in the Coliseum in Los Angeles, a reporter came in and said, "Guess what happened! One of the boys broke the American record in the 400-meter hurdles." Great! But he didn't win the race. Someone asked who *did* beat him. Josh Culbreath ran 50.4, but he didn't win either. Eddie Southern ran 49.7 to defeat Josh Culbreath. That was seven-tenths of a second better than the world's record—but that didn't win either. "Well, who beat Eddie?" was the next question. "Glenn Davis did it in 49.5."

I am convinced that if anyone is going to become great in life or in sports, he has to welcome competition, to welcome someone, a pioneer, who will set the standard high. I don't think that most people compete enough; they give up too easily, they level off, they let their personal standards dominate them and they never press on. Would that we had the competitive spirit of Paul the apostle, who said, "I run in such a way, as not without aim; I box in such a way, as not beating the air" (1 Cor. 9:26 NASB). He ran to win. He also said, "Do you not know that those who run in a race all run, but one receives the prize? Run in such a way that you may obtain it" (v. 24 NKJV). Paul was a fierce competitor. It was what made him a great man of God. You've *got* to compete! It is tragic in this day, when there is so much evil in the world, that so many of us refuse competition. It is time for us to re-evaluate ourselves and go on to the heights we should reach.

If a man is going to be what he ought to be, he's got to be willing to *put out just a little bit more*. Now I know that this might sound trite, but the more I watch great men, the more I see the processes by which men achieve their goals, the more I am convinced that it is the willingness to put out just a little bit more that makes the difference. In many a race I have seen that there isn't a gigantic difference between victory or defeat; more often it is simply by the smallest margin that a man is named the winner. This holds true in all of life. The difference between a saint and a sinner is not as great as people may think. The difference between a PhD in school and the fellow who didn't quite make it is that little bit more study, that extra page that a man turns every night as he burns the midnight oil. The difference in business is not always that one man is more gifted than another. It is that one man puts out a little bit more. So often people think that a champion has a tremendous edge over everyone else. They think he is 99 percent perfect as against the other fellow's 50 percent. Actually the difference is more like 98.8 percent over 98.7 percent. It's that small degree of putting out a little bit more that does it.

I wish I could convey to you what I have seen in Olympic contests. I have seen boys blaze down a broad-jump runway, go off the toe board into the pit and look back expecting to receive the roar of the crowd signifying victory, only to see a red flag waving. They had fouled by an eighth of an inch. You go up to a boy like that, put your arm around him and tell him it doesn't make any difference, he only fouled by an eighth of an inch. He will tell you that he didn't even place—the greatest broad jumper in the world didn't even place, because of that little foul. I remember watching Don Bragg and Ronnie Morris, both pole-vaulters, in the 1956 Olympic tryouts. I'll never forget Don Bragg, a big 200-pound boy with arms as big as my legs, as he roared down the takeoff. He had been bothered by a pulled muscle, but he went up and over the crossbar by about 6 inches, and started down only to look up to see the pole come through and knock the crossbar off—and he was off the Olympic team. Ronnie Morris did the same thing. He waited twenty minutes for his last trial. All of the other events were over. The crowd of 40,000 people was spellbound, waiting to see who would make the team in the pole vault. Ronnie waited while the wind shifted, started two or three times, stopped and came back. Finally, the wind behind him, he roared down the take-off, planted his pole, drove his feet and swung his hips up and through. It was one of the greatest jumps of his life. He sailed over the crossbar by about six inches. As the crowd roared, Ronnie started his descent. He landed in the sawdust and then started to jump up with a happy smile of victory— he was on the Olympic team—and the crossbar fell off into his hands. His pole had come through. Do you know how much it takes to throw a pole back? Just a flick of the finger, that's all—but that little bit more that he failed to put into his jump was the difference between making the Olympic team or not. He might have been a world's champion. A little bit more at a crucial moment can make all the difference.

I have seen boys miss the Olympic team just like that in three Olympic contests. In 1948 I watched George Walker fail to make the 400-meter hurdle team by a quarter of an inch. I saw Harrison Dillard just barely touch the top of a hurdle and stop and not make the Olympic team. In

1956, Rafer Johnson edged out a boy by an inch and a half in the broad jump. Freddy Dwyer looked to his left and Don Bowden passed him on the right by six inches in the 1,500 meters. And in the Olympic Games in 1948, Emil Zatopek, one of the greatest runners in the world, was defeated by a few feet in the 5,000 meters by Gaston Reiff of Belgium, simply because he didn't put out that little bit more at the right time. It's that extra chin-up every day and that extra push-up, it's that extra lap around the track, that extra five minutes a person puts into his workout, into his schoolwork or into his home life or business that makes the difference in his life.

Now sometimes winning requires that we do a little bit *less*. I was giving this speech to a group of teachers and a big roly-poly girl, who must have weighed 210 pounds, came up to me afterwards and said, "Mr. Richards, I don't agree with you." And I said, "Why? I don't understand." She replied, "Well, it's the little bit more that made me fat." She should have eaten a little *less*, not *more*. The fellow with the heart attack will say that it's the little bit more he did that caused it; he should have exerted himself less. You've got to have the sense to realize that sometimes you must do more, sometimes less.

This is illustrated by the story of a fellow who, in a debate over whether smoking and drinking hurt a fellow in athletics, said that he didn't feel smoking and drinking hurt him enough, that he would rather indulge in them than take the joy out of living. A second runner—and a scientist— made a study and found that when an athlete smoked a certain number of cigarettes and drank a certain quantity of liquor, it would affect his time on the track—as much as six inches in a hundred yards—and that multiplied over a distance of 10,000 meters or so, it would make a difference of two, three, or four yards. But the first fellow stuck to it; said that he didn't think that was necessarily true. What a fantastic thing it was that, in the next year, this same man was in three races—the mile, the three-mile and the 5,000-meter—and he lost by about six inches each time. All three would have been world's records had he made it. If one is going to be the kind of person he ought to be, I say this: In the good and creative things, you've got to put out a little bit more, and in the negative things that tear down, you've got to be willing to indulge a little bit less. This is what makes greatness in living.

Again, if you want to be the person you ought to be, *you've got to be a good sport.* The more I analyze sports, the more I am convinced that it has a certain basic moral precept underwriting it that gives it its meaning and purpose. Sportsmanship is fundamental to the sports world. Eliminate it and you almost eliminate sports entirely. Sports without sportsmanship simply cannot function; there must be those rules and concepts of behavior on the athletic field that give sports its meaning. The boys who are "playing dirty," the boys who are trying to break the rules and sneak by without letting the officials know that they are doing it, are poor risks in life. I have seen boys use their arms illegally in football, I have seen boys grab others' clothing in basketball, and I have seen fellows try to develop secret devices for breaking rules. But I say this: Moral behavior carries off the field into life, and the person who is guilty of such infractions on the field will invariably be guilty of similar infractions of the laws of society. Being a good sport is irrevocably bound up with greatness in life.

Bob Gutowski and I were jumping in the Melbourne Olympic Games. I had rather a difficult time qualifying, for I had injured a tendon in my left foot and it was a little bit sore. The crossbar was set at 13 feet, 1½ inches, and I didn't check on it. A boy from Puerto Rico had jumped just before I was to make my jump, and because he was only seventeen years old, the officials wanted to measure the height for a new Australian junior record. In the process of measuring it, they moved the standards forward, which brought the crossbar in too close. I didn't check, and went roaring down the straightaway. When I went up, because the crossbar was in too close, I hit it and knocked it off. Well, the second time I checked it very meticulously, went back, cleared it by about three feet—but a gust of wind blew my pole into the crossbar and knocked it off again. Talk about tension and pressure! Here I was the defending champion in this Olympic event, with just one jump left. As I went back for the third time, I actually began to tremble a little bit. If I slipped off my grip, if I did something wrong, it was conceivable that I could have missed 13 feet and been out of the Games. I was nervous and I remember before going back that I asked the officials if they had moved the standards. They said no, that they were exactly right. I went back and had just started to go when Bob Gutowski, my companion for the USA team, came up to me and said, "Bob, they have moved the standards again." Well, it unnerved me, and I went back and discovered that once again in measuring for a new Australian junior record they had moved the standards in and I would have undoubtedly missed for the third time and would have been out of the Games. But because Bob Gutowski told me, I changed the standards, cleared it and later went on to jump 14 feet, 11½ inches. But here is the significant thing. I beat Bob Gutowski by one inch. In other words, if Bob hadn't told me, he would have been the Olympic Games winner instead of me. I would have gone out in disgrace and shame and Bob Gutowski would have won. Now, you might say that Bob lost because he was a good sport. But the next year Gutowski came back to tie me in the Millrose Games with a jump of 15 feet, 6 inches, and went on during the spring to break Cornelius Warmerdan's record of 15 feet, 7¾ inches, a record that I had tried to beat all through my vaulting career.

I believe there is a relationship between being a good sport and being the success that you want to be. For me, the definition of sportsmanship has something spiritual about it, something of the Golden Rule: Do unto others as you would have them do unto you. Would that we could practice that sportsmanship, that Golden Rule, in every realm of life. What if men would just be good sports, live and let live, not be prejudiced, try to understand the other fellow's point of view, follow the Golden Rule? This is a cardinal principle of sports, and it is so relevant to all of life.

Lastly, you have to *maintain your enthusiasm*. If a person is going to be the kind of person he wants to be or ought to be, this is a must. Now I have seen this again and again in the sports world. Maintaining enthusiasm is the hardest thing in training. Sometimes you go out on the field and are tired, worn-out, you don't have the zip—and it is so easy to let down, just go through the motions, but not really pour yourself into it and get something out of your workout. I've stood at the end of the runway many times and wondered what in the world I was doing out here—I've jumped so many times. This is what can happen. And when you lose your enthusiasm you work less, and if you work less, you fail, and if you fail, you lose your enthusiasm and you work less and lose more enthusiasm. When you get yourself caught in this terrible, vicious cycle, you start down. Somehow this enthusiasm must be maintained because as enthusiasm grows, a person works harder, and from hard work comes the success every person needs.

I have a little boy eight years old. Please don't think that I am trying to force my boy to be a pole vaulter; I just buy him track shoes, track pants, and dig a pit for him, get him a pole and standards and have him work out with me every day. I'm not forcing him to be a pole vaulter; he can be whatever he wants to be. I just like to lend a *little* influence. I had him jumping one day; he cleared the bar at about 4 feet, 6 inches and I said to him, "Bobby, you can jump 5 feet easily." So I raised it up to 5 feet, 6 inches and he tried and missed, tried again and missed, tried again, missed again—until finally he came up to me and took my hand and said, "Daddy, let's go put the shot." You see what had happened? He had failed enough so that his enthusiasm was just gone. So I took the crossbar and moved it down to 4 feet, 8 inches. He made that. I moved it to 4 feet 10, a little bit at a time, and he made that. I raised it to 5 feet and he made that. He wound up that day making 5 feet, 8 inches, the best height he had ever attained. But you see, it was with each success that his enthusiasm began to grow and he began to drive harder and to do better.

Life is like that. If we try to go too high, we frustrate ourselves. Many and many a time I have found that if you try the world's record, you just can't make it—you become more frustrated with every miss. But if you start it at about 14 feet and go up an inch at a time, pretty soon you are at the world's record. Just remember this: an inch at a time and eventually you come to the world's record. This is very important for all of life: It isn't the point where you are that matters, it's the direction in which you are heading. So long as you are going up, even if it is just a quarter of an inch or a tenth of a second, your enthusiasm need not wane.

Incidentally, do you know what the word *enthusiasm* really means? It comes from the Greek *entheos*, which means "in-Godded." In other words, it really means that you have God in your life and that He has inspired you to reach the heights. I have noticed in the sports world again and again that many boys have as the central core of their motivation a divine relationship with God. I could mention so many of them—Milt Campbell, Rafer Johnson, Doak Walker, Don Moomaw, and Otto Graham, Deacon Dan Towler, Gary Demarisk, Alvin Dark, Carl Erskine, Billy Wade—all great fellows in the world of sports, who have prayed. They find in their religious devotion an inner spring of enthusiasm that helps them in life. They have found the truth in the Bible's statement that "they that wait upon the LORD shall renew their strength; they shall mount up with wings as eagles; they shall run, and not be weary; and they shall walk, and not faint" (Isa. 40:31).

When I was sixteen, I was converted and found God. I began to study harder, I began to make friends, I began to train harder. I never amounted to anything prior to that, but finding God was the fountainhead of all kinds of great things in my life. What I am saying is this: If you would be the kind of person you know you ought to be, you must analyze yourself, recognize your weaknesses and work on them; you must welcome competition; you must put out that little bit more; you must be a good sport, win or lose; you must have enthusiasm and—lastly and above all—take God into your life, for in Him is the source of all great things in the world. And with Him inspiring and motivating and lifting and empowering, you can reach the great heights of life.

# RESPONSE TO THE CHALLENGE

D<br>r. Arnold Toynbee, in his amazing ten-volume history of civilization, says that you can measure civilization by studying the responses of the people of history to the great challenges they have had to face; that history is only the record of how they faced one crisis after another. As we have responded, so has history taken its course. When we have responded negatively, progress has slowed down, cultures have disintegrated, empires have collapsed. When we have responded positively, mankind has leaped ahead, art, music, religion and industry have flourished, life has been more abundant. The way we react to our challenges determines the destiny of our lives, our country and our world.

I hardly need repeat the well-known statement that we live in the most challenging hour of all time. I think that's obvious to anyone who knows history or who knows the gigantic problems that men are grappling with today. Depending upon the responses that you and I make, so will go the next ten, twenty, thirty years, if there are those thirty years. I couldn't possibly analyze *all* of the enormous challenges of our time, but may I list what I think are the primary ones that you and I are facing in today's world?

Number one—this may sound strange to some of you, but to me it is the most important challenge—*there is the challenge of using the genius of man for the creative things of life rather than for the destructive things of life.* This one hit me not long ago while reading Albert Einstein's book *Out of My Later Years.* Here was a man, perhaps the greatest scientist of all history, saying words to the effect that it was his hope that his theories would be used for the betterment of mankind, and his chief sorrow was to see some of his ideas, which had led to the development of hydrogen energy and the hydrogen bomb, used not in their creative intent, but used for destruction. Einstein went on to say that it seems as though there is a bent in culture that uses the great genius of mankind for that which maims and hurts. I saw that illustrated not long ago. I was talking with a young teacher who showed me a switchblade knife made out of three popsicle sticks and two rubber bands. A little eight-year-old boy had made this thing; as I saw the ingenuity involved in making that switchblade knife, I couldn't help but think to myself, "Well, we don't want for genius." Latent within the minds of thousands are tremendous ideas and ingenious methods; the trouble is that they are bent in the wrong direction. The first real challenge of modern history is to use our genius for the creative, for that which builds up mankind instead of that which tears down.

Secondly—and this is a minor one—*there is the challenge of maintaining health in a day of mechanization.* This one struck me not long ago at Purdue University, while I was there giving a talk. We were held up in the street by a car in front of us, a car waiting for a boy to come out of a fraternity house; eventually the boy sauntered out, got into the car, drove fifty yards around the corner, got out and went to his second-period class. I couldn't help but think of how this illustrates one of the dilemmas of modern man. We have push-button gadgets, mechanization to the point that we are losing our physical dynamic. We are losing the virility that is so indispensable in building happiness and creativity in life. I met a man in Chicago not long ago who was all excited about a push-button gadget he had; he would push a button and the television picture would change; he would push another button and the sound would go up, another and the sound would go down. He was most enthusiastic about this thing. I may be a physical education bug, but I couldn't help but wonder at people who wouldn't even get up to change the TV picture; they just sit there getting wider and wider and wider.

We should realize that health is the predication upon which great things in life are built. A nation that is not strong physically, or a person who is not strong physically, cannot accomplish great things. I will go so far as to say this—and it may hurt some folks—but I believe that there is a relationship between physical discipline and the discipline of the mind and the spirit and the emotions. The person who is not physically fit is indicating a basic pattern of weakness in certain areas, and I think that when a nation becomes weak, something bad has happened to the fiber of the people.

Thirdly, *there is the challenge to maintain an emphasis upon the total personality in a day of specialization.* The more and more I see this, the more I am convinced that sometimes we see people only as functions, rather than as sacred entities with intrinsic worth. Nowadays a man is thought of in terms of a laboring personality, or as a soldier, or a scientist. Each and every one of us is more than a function. Each and every one of us is an emotional, moral, mental, aesthetic, spiritual being, and you don't deal adequately with the problems of men until you recognize that these facets must be developed. If there is one ingenious principle of the American public school system, to me, it is this: the emphasis upon building a total personality, not just a being crammed with facts that can put out Sputniks into space. That we will do, and that is important; but how much more important is the building of a person who can love and live and adjust and give and take and create. This, to me, is the fundamental principle that has made the American public school system what it is. I hope we never lose it. We *must* maintain that emphasis upon the total personality.

Fourthly, *there is the challenge of maintaining personal relationships in an impersonal urban society.* As I go into urban areas, I am more and more impressed with the fact that we seem to be trying to depersonalize everyone, and in the process we are dehumanizing people. I had a church in Long Beach, California, not long ago, and I used to go out and make calls. One day I knocked on a door, and as I didn't know quite where I was, I asked the lady who opened the door, "Do you know where Mr. and Mrs. So-and-So live?" She looked at me and said that she had never heard of them. She had lived right next door to the people I sought; she had been there for two years, and she didn't even know their names! And *they* didn't know her name.

I was on a committee on juvenile delinquency, one of a group of ministers, sports figures and police officers. A lot of the youngsters were there, and we were exchanging ideas. The outstanding juvenile expert of Long Beach stood up and told a little story about his boy, who had a paper route with forty customers. The boy used to come home every night and talk about a Mrs. Washington. The father couldn't understand why, but one day the boy came home late and he took him to task: "Why are you so late? Why aren't you home on time?" He said, "Why, Dad, I was talking with Mrs. Washington." "Why do you spend so much time talking with her?" When he got the answer he was shocked; his boy said, "Why, Dad, she *talked* to me; she spoke to me!" Out of the forty customers on the boy's route, only one had ever spoken to him. You see things like this and can understand what this father had in mind when he said to us, "How many of those people on that paper route could be sitting around this table with us talking about what's wrong with our young people?" There is only one thing that is ever going to solve this problem, and that is people taking a genuine interest in young people. I have come to believe that the old biblical question, "Am I my brother's keeper?" has an unusual relevance for today's world. In a day of loneliness, in a day of increasing socialized structures, we need to break through the walls of our impersonal institutions and meet *people*, and help them.

It is part of every great religious philosophy, and it is one of the great challenges of our time.

Fifth, *there is the challenge to maintain brotherhood in a day of prejudice.* I need not stress this one too much. I am quite sure that you are aware of the racial tensions in America and in the world. Every headline, every radio report—yesterday's, today's—is filled with this gnawing problem that is eating away at the heart of democracy. I had an interesting conversation recently with Dr. Howard Thurman, of Boston University. We were talking about racial integration and racial problems, and Dr. Thurman, a wise preacher, likened it all to a man who had a daughter with a club foot. He took this daughter to a doctor and waited in the anteroom. Pretty soon screams were heard from the doctor's office. People in the anteroom couldn't understand why the father was so happy about it. Finally one man nudged him and asked him how he could sit there smiling while his daughter was going through such pain. He said, "Sir, you don't understand. This is the first time she has ever felt anything in her foot." Dr. Thurman went on to say that all over the world the conscience of man is being aroused, that in this age-old problem, at last, the basic principles of democracy and the Christian heritage are beginning to be felt, that people are really beginning to wrestle with this problem. He said that it would be solved, but not without some piercing screams as the conscience of man battles with the problem. The world is almost won scientifically; it will be possible, in a few years, to go around the world in ten to twelve hours, perhaps in eight. The world is that small—yet it is torn asunder by prejudice. Not only racially, but religiously, and politically; the real challenge in this day is to maintain brotherhood, to stress the essential humanity of humanity. It is a hard one, but it is one of the great challenges that each and every one of us faces.

Sixth, *there is the economic challenge.* It is the problem of feeding the world and meeting global economic need. I was in India a few years ago. Coming out of my hotel room, I ran down the steps, grabbed my bags; late for a plane, I jumped into a cab, and at that moment out of the corner of my eye I saw a lot of human beings asleep on the sidewalk. I backed out of the cab and looked around; as far as I could see on the right and on the left, I saw people sleeping on the sidewalks. I found out later that there are thousands of people in Calcutta who have no home other than the sidewalk. Go through Hong Kong and see people there sleeping sitting up, and get a sense of the tremendous population increase in the world. I need not tell you that a whole new nation is born every year. Sixty-three million people were born last year, and many of them are literally starving to death. They want an economic answer. To talk platitudes to them, even to talk of liberty and freedom to people who have known nothing but hunger, want and slavery to economic needs, is to talk foolishly. It must be met; the real challenge of our time is whether it will be met with the creative genius of the individual, or by the state. It all boils down to whether individuals can rise to the occasion, to whether, in a free society, individuals can with faith begin to work out their problems. It is a tremendous question and it involves all of us. I know the tendency is to let the state solve the problem; therein lies the real crisis. *We must solve it with creative individuals helping and working together.*

Seventh, *there is the challenge of meeting the dynamic of Communism.* I put this one next to the economic challenge because I've just seen it in Moscow; I've just seen those young intellectuals marching down the street with outstretched arms, shouting, "We are out to win the world. We're out to win the world!" They are young men and women, fresh out of school. Their leadership is not being utilized effectively; because of some egotistical twist, they go off into Communism. You can see them in Bombay and other places, eyes flashing with hatred, inciting mob riots, disseminating hatred. You see this thing and you begin to realize that there is a deadly dynamic to Communism. I can't understand it; I suppose you have read *Das Kapital*; you know all about it! It is nonsense, in many respects, but the fantastic thing is to see it take hold. People are passionately committed to it. I don't think it will ever be wished away. I don't believe that it will be bombed away. It will only be defeated by a greater passion, or a greater way of life, for a system greater with meaning. Again, it involves all of us. It is a question of passion, not of theory but of dynamic, and of belief and what a person is living for—a question of purpose. It goes to the heart of moral philosophy. Meeting the dynamic of Communism is one of the real issues of our time.

And lastly, closely related to this, *there is the challenge of maintaining a spiritual perspective in a day of materialism.* Not only Communist materialism, but a more subtle form of materialism, eats away the real genius of man. I am not just talking religion here, but I am saying that every great principle of democracy grows out of a spiritual framework. You don't have ideas in isolation; every idea has a root. And I maintain that the sacredness of the human personality, the idea of the rights of every person, the concept that every individual has ingenious creativity, are all rooted in a Judeo-Christian heritage. These are part of our culture. Such a spiritual perspective is essential. I think that the only thing that can meet Communism successfully is a point of view that insists that moral values are written into the heart of the universe, that truth triumphs over falsehood, that goodness triumphs over evil, that love triumphs over hate, that there is a purpose to life; what we need is not just a meaningless dialectic weaving to and fro wiping out whatever it will, but a thought process that writes moral values into the process of history. To say this requires a spiritual perspective. My personal conviction is that religion is a large part of the problem. I mean *real* religion, not the kind that is concerned with someone being holier than somebody else, or with someone having a little bit cuter idea or someone having a little nicer phrase than somebody else, or a better creed or dogma. How tragic this is! Our world simply is not concerned at all about how many angels can dance on the point of a needle; it isn't concerned with cute theological phrases; our world needs something to live by.

This reminds me of the story of two men walking in a mental institution. One fellow nudged the other and asked, "What are you in here for?" The other one said, "Why, I took a gun and shot a hole in my head." The first one said, "You did? Why, that's why I'm in here too. I took a gun and shot two holes in my head." The other replied, "That's what I don't like about you—that holier-than-thou attitude." There is a sense in which it's true. We have been so concerned with being holier than somebody else that we are just shooting holes in our heads. We have seven million chronic alcoholics in America. One in three homes has a divorce. One out of thirteen of us is a mental case. Juvenile crime is increasing. Tranquilizer pills, aspirins by the tons, are being consumed. In the last ten years, the world has spent over one trillion dollars on weapons of war, which are obsolete as soon as they are made. Fear grips the world. If ever there was a time when religion needed to be made real, when people needed love, faith, trust, it's now. To make religion live in human life may be the greatest challenge of all.

And how do we respond to these challenges? We can respond negatively. That is *so* easy! We can respond by saying that "There is really nothing that I can do: after all, I am just one little person in a vast world of social forces and struggle for power: what can I do?" It is always the wail of the soul, "What can I do in the midst of such terrific organizations?" If you are ever prone to doubt what you can do as an individual, think of Karl Marx writing a *Das Kapital* by candlelight. Think of two little lone disciples—unknown to the world—Lenin and Trotsky; in less than forty years these three men have won half the world to Communism. Or, on the creative side, think of men like Moses and David, of men like Jesus, who stood at the heart of a society ripped with struggle for power. Think of a man like Abraham Lincoln, of other individuals who have stood on their principles in the critical hours of history and have changed the world.

There are youngsters today who will change the world tomorrow. We must encourage them, build in them true ideas, and we must remember that ideas are no good at all except in the minds of individuals. Causes have no emotion at all except in the emotion and passion of individuals. If we will work with the minds of young boys and girls, with their emotions and values, we and they can alter human history. Ultimately, everything depends upon the individual. Don't respond by saying there is nothing you can do. Don't respond with the hysteria of fear. The world has too much of this already. In the London Art Gallery, not long ago, I walked into a room and saw a great big "modern art" thing with a big eye leering out of the world. Behind this there was a glob of hair, and behind this a glob of color and a leg going out one way and an arm and hand another. I looked at it and I couldn't make rhyme nor reason of what the artist was trying to communicate. Finally, I went to a guard nearby and asked, "What in the world is that man trying to say?" He said, "Why, sir, can't you tell? That is a picture of a woman gone all to pieces." The more I thought of that picture, the more I thought that maybe modern art does serve a function in portraying the jangled emotions of our lives and in showing how we are going all to pieces. We can't respond that way. We need cool, rational thinking in people. Nor can we respond with the old philosophy of "Eat, drink and be merry, for tomorrow we die." That way lies disaster.

May I speak for a moment from the world of sports? I think sports come to grips with life; I think that in some of these great stories you can see into the heart of human society. In sports, the first demand is that the athlete respond quickly. Immediately!

I think of Herb Elliott, a great miler from Australia. Back in Australia, about a year or two ago, Herb Elliott had a broken foot; he hadn't been running for several months. He watched John Landy run the mile under four minutes. He went up to Coach Percy Cerutty, one of the best coaches in Australia, and he said, "Mr. Cerutty, I want to run the mile in less than four minutes." Cerutty looked at him and said, "Son, do you know what it takes to run a mile under four minutes? Do you know what it is to run until you can hardly stand up, to suck in hot air until you're almost unconscious? Do you know what it is to run that kind of a race?" Elliott said, "I don't care what it takes; I want to run the mile under four minutes." The coach said, "OK, come out to the track tomorrow." But Cerutty didn't put him on the track; he took him out to a beach nearby, ran him uphill on the sand and ran him over boulders and rocks. He ran him over the most difficult obstacle course he could find. The kid kept running; he wouldn't give up. Less than one year later, I watched him run the mile in 3:57.8 in the Coliseum, and recently he ran 3:54.5, to smash the world's record. A nineteen- or twenty-year-old boy! That's what can happen when a man responds, when he gets a vision, when he believes that there is something that he can do. With this passion—how I wish I could describe it—there is something that integrates everything a boy or girl has, and it goes out into one endeavor.

I was in Kingsburg, California, a little while back, working with some boys after giving a speech at the high school. I noticed a tall, lean kid, who was president of the student body, working out; I said, "You ought to go out for the decathlon; you have lots of ability." This serious young boy looked me in the eye and he said, "That is exactly what I aim to do. I want to become a great decathlon man."

Eight months later that boy beat me in the Pan-American Olympic Games, and three months after that he broke Bob Mathias's world's record. I was with him in Moscow. I'll never forget it. I watched this boy battling with the man who had broken his world's record, Kuznetsov of Russia. They had come down to the javelin event; Rafer Johnson (the boy from Kingsburg) was only 204 points ahead, and Kuznetsov's strong event was the javelin and he was about 10 feet beyond Rafer, who had thrown twice. Kuznetsov was at 214 and Rafer was at 205. I watched Rafer go back for his next throw. I could see his white teeth set, his muscles trembling. It was near dark. The crowd was so tense that you could have heard a pin drop. It was more than just an athletic contest; you could almost see the spirit of the two peoples involved here. Rafer went down, bent in and with a terrific "uhhhhhhh," he let that javelin go and the thing leveled off where Kuznetsov's flag was in the ground. It leveled off and went out, out, out—and landed 238 feet away. The Russian crowd went "ohhhhhh!" Rafer had broken the world's record; Kuznetsov was defeated. That is what I mean by the ability to respond. Immediately! To do something about a challenge. Goethe put it so beautifully in these words, "Are you in earnest? Choose this very moment. Beginning has magic, power, boldness in it. The mind grows heated." Respond *now*; you don't know what you can do until you have made an immediate response to a challenge.

We must respond with *embodied faith*. It is so easy to talk about faith; in fact there are probably two hundred books on the bookstands today written by people talking about faith, or about positive thinking, or "magic in believing." They are great books, but I think that 99 percent of those authors are talking about what 1 percent of the people already have. Faith isn't something you can kick around, like a syllogism. It isn't a game of intellectual chess. Faith is something that quivers on your lip, something that trembles in the human hand, something that you act upon; it is emotion, grounded, incorporated, *embodied*. It is something you live by; so often people talk about it, but they don't really have it.

It reminds me of a football game I once saw. I watched the University of Illinois play Minnesota a few years back, when I was in high school. I had gotten into the locker rooms. Illinois hadn't won a game that year; they were really down. In fact, I don't think they were even building character that year, their morale was that low. Minnesota hadn't *lost* a game. Big Bill Daley, an all-American prospect at 240 pounds, was the line average; they were a great team. They would slaughter Illinois, according to the experts, by 30 points. When I looked at them in the locker room, I felt that they were beaten before they went out on the field. The Illinois boys were just going through the motions. They didn't believe they could do it—all but one man named Alex Agase, who very quietly went around grabbing them by their jerseys, pulling them up to within two inches from his eyes and saying, "We can beat them! *We can beat them!*" Pretty soon that cry became a roar in the locker room. Now Alex Agase would never win an oratorical contest; yet soon, eye-ball to eye-ball, the boys were saying, "We can beat them, we can beat them, *we can beat them!*" They believed they could do it. They went roaring out onto the field; they played not over their heads but within their heads. Sure, they had cotton in their mouths; sure, they perspired; sure, they hurt. But Alex blocked a kick for one touchdown, then stole the ball from all-American Bill Daley for another touchdown. They upset Minnesota by 16 to 7—the greatest upset of the year, the experts said.

What would happen in the world if people like you and me would really go to work together, as a team, and say, "We can beat them. We can triumph over ignorance. We can triumph over the forces of evil. We can triumph over brutal force and materialism. We can beat them, not with just killing and slaughter, but by outliving them and out-creating them, by producing a greater dynamic!" I think of one who said, "In all these things we are more than conquerors through him that loved us" (Rom. 8:37). Paul changed a pagan world because he dared to believe that he could beat that pagan world and its ideas. I think that this embodied faith is what the world most needs. Real faith that it can be done. Faith not only in ourselves, but in other people.

Carl Erskine is a good friend of mine. He told me once about his greatest experience in baseball. In a World Series, Brooklyn was ahead two games to one; the score was 5 to 2. A man walked up to the plate; Carl walked him. Another fellow got up, and Carl walked him. Then big Johnnie Mize (they used to call him The Cat) stepped up with two men on. Carl put one in the wrong spot, and Johnnie lifted the ball into the cheap seats of Brooklyn Stadium. The score was tied. Carl said to me, "Bob, I can't tell you how I felt at that moment—I knew I had let my teammates down, that in that crucial moment I hadn't come up to what I should have been." Charlie Dressen came off the bench and said, "Carl, how do you feel?" He said, "I think I am all right." Carl told me, "Actually, Bob, if he had pulled me out of that game, I don't think I would ever have come back, I was just that low." Dressen reached up and took him by the arm and said, "Carl, you're my man; I am leaving you in. You can do it!" He turned his back and walked back to the dugout. Carl said, "Bob, to know that he believed in me, to know that my teammates were behind me—well, I knew I *had* to come through." He retired the next sixteen men in order, and three days later they won the series behind his brilliant pitching.

Now you'll say, "Oh, it's just another story." But I wonder if you don't get life in its deepest dimensions in that story. I wonder how many men have been changed by just such a touch on the shoulder? When I was a boy of sixteen, a young minister put his hand on my shoulder and said, "Bob, you ought to be a minister for the Lord." It changed my whole life! I wonder how many people have been transformed with that touch of faith? I think this may be the great need in our homes today. Instead of the tension and gnawing, we need this touch of faith. I wonder if it isn't what needs to happen between parents and children: the touch of a parent's hand saying, "I believe in you." I wonder if this is not the schoolteachers' greatest work—not so much to disseminate factual knowledge, but to instill in the youngsters a sense of the faith we have in them. I wonder how many teachers have saved the world, by that touch of faith? How the world needs it! If only we could believe in *people*!

On my recent trip to Russia, I saw a lot of bad things; I could write another book telling you about those bad things. But when I start talking about the good people whom I saw over there, nobody wants to listen! Why? Is it because nobody wants to believe in humanity anymore? Maybe what the world needs more than anything else is a touch on the shoulder with somebody saying, "I believe in you, I believe in you!" Something like the feeling Jesus had for Peter when He said, "I have prayed for you." Embodied faith in human relationships! The touch on the shoulder, the faith that lives in action!

We must respond to these challenges with courage. I haven't said anything new there, have I? Courage is as old as Greek philosophy. Five hundred years before Jesus, the Greeks made it a cardinal principle of their system of ethics. We talk courage, but we know not what it is. Here is what I think it is. It's an all-American halfback playing pro football, going through the line for a terrific tackle and getting a concussion above his right ear. The all-American can't even catch a ball, after that concussion. The ball slips through his fingers; he stumbles over his own feet when he tries to run. But he has courage; he fights through it and rebuilds his coordination. He was Elroy Hirsch, who went back into pro football and for eight years after the injury was the greatest end in the game. They call him "Crazy Legs Hirsch," and they respect him! Or I think of a boy pitching a baseball; he leans in with all he's got and follows through, there is a crack of the bat, a blur of white and he is hit in the eye. He faced a life of semi-blindness, but he has courage, and he beats it. In high faith and courage, he goes back on the mound; hesitant now to follow through, he *forces* himself to lean into the pitch and follow through again. He is Herb Score—one of the greatest in baseball.

I was in New York recently, interviewing Junius Kellogg, the boy who was an "honorable mention" all-American basketball player at Manhattan College. He saved college basketball by reporting the gamblers to the D. A. You may have read the story. An automobile smashup broke his neck and left him paralyzed for life. I talked to him as he sat in a wheelchair; I listened to him say, "You know, I used to be a song and dance man. The dance is gone, but they will never take away my song." Or there is Roy Campanella, telling us that he has everything to live for. From his wheelchair he is helping hundreds to go on. That, my friend, is courage!

I think of the Babe. You know about Babe Didrikson, who won two gold medals in the Olympic Games. She was all-American in softball, basketball, horseback riding, tennis, golf, swimming, and then—cancer. At the height of her career, cancer! She called in her pastor the day before she died and said, "Pray a little harder, I'm getting a little closer." The pastor prayed, and left. I played golf with her husband, and he told me the story himself of how she called him to her bedside, took him by the hand and said, "Honey, I hope you will find someone to love you as much as I have loved you." And then, as he cried like a baby, she gripped his hand as tightly as she could and said, "Now, honey, don't take on so. While I've been in the hospital, I have learned one thing. A moment of happiness is a lifetime, and I have had a lot of happiness. I have had a lot of it." That's courage! It goes to the heart of things. To stress the quality of life rather than just quantity, to meet life's greatest tragedy with a smile, saying, "I have had a lot of great moments of happiness"—this is courage! Search the pages of philosophy, and you will find nothing greater than that statement. This is what I think courage is, and I believe that every one of us, in some way or another, must meet life with this principle. You've got to meet it so, when you are hurt; we've got to go back into the fight and keep on going, keep on pitching, to conquer the tragedy and live a creative, useful life. We must stress the quality, the moments of happiness. That's what makes courage.

Lastly, we must meet *the challenges with commitment.* This is interwoven in every aspect of life. I have seen it in sports. The greatest athletes whom I know, pray. In this world of muscle and bone, I have heard them breathe a prayer that God will help them. I have seen them kneel down in locker rooms and say, "God, help me come back." I have seen men, almost nauseated, praying, "Help me do my best." I have talked to fellows like Doak Walker and others, who have told me that they never go on the field until they pray for help. I think of a kid in Melbourne, Australia; I sat next to him in a church service down there. When I should have been praying, I peeked out of the corner of my eye and listened to him repeat the Lord's Prayer. A year later he was the first boy in America to run the mile under four minutes. You'll never convince me that there isn't a relationship between Don Bowden sitting in that little church in Melbourne and what he did on the track. I remember Maxie Truex, a little 5-feet 6-inch, 129-pounder, who said to me, "Bob, with God's help I am going to break every long distance record in America." And the very next year he did it! You'll never convince me that he ran with just his 129 pounds; he runs with everything he has—heart, faith, will, determination. I think of Jimmy Brewer, a high school kid, who jumped 15 feet. I saw him do it in Phoenix. I used to think 15 feet was rather high; when I did it they thought it was great. Now high school boys are doing it. I watched this boy work out four hours a day, nine months of the year. He was offered a big $500 silver trophy as the outstanding scholastic athlete of the year and turned it down because it was offered by a brewery. I wondered what kind of a boy he was; I knew when he said, "Bob, my faith means more to me than anything."

I could go on and tell you about so many others, but let me sum it up by saying that perhaps the problems at the periphery of life are due to the fact that man is off center, and that, if he can only find himself in cosmic relationship to God, these problems will be solved. I hope that you can respond to that challenge. I hope you will respond to it right now, with an embodied faith, with a spiritual commitment. I hope you will find the greatest challenge ever given to man, given in two words: "Follow me." I pray that you will respond to every moment of great inspiration and challenge, but above all that you will respond to this "Follow me," the greatest challenge of all human history.

**Bob Richards** is a champion all-around athlete, a former holder of the Olympic pole vault record, the Olympic gold medalist in men's pole vault for 1952 and 1956, and former director of the Wheaties Sports Federation. In 1958 he was also the first athlete to appear on the front of a Wheaties cereal box. He currently runs Olympian Ranch with his wife, Joan, in Gordon, Texas, where they breed champion miniature horses.

# Change the way you think . . . and you can change your life.

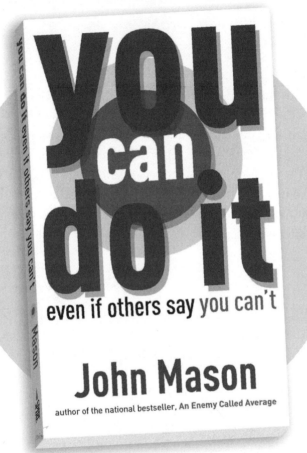

Find the inspiration for pursuing your dreams, right between these pages. You can live a fruitful and fulfilling life, believing that God will provide the means to accomplish the impossible. And the best part is—you can start right now!